A rare drawing
by *Nancy*'s artist, Ernie Bushmiller.

100% OF CRAIG YOE'S PROCEEDS GO TO...

THE CHILDREN AFFECTED
BY AIDS FOUNDATION
AND
THE MILT GROSS FUND
(a charity of
the National Cartoonists Society
that assists cartoonists in need
and their families).

Illustration by Milt Gross, 1926.

Art by Rube Goldberg
and Bill Holman.

ELEMENTARY, MY DEAR READER!

FACT! THE *MARX BROTHERS'* NAMES, *CHICO, HARPO,* AND *GROUCHO,* WERE INSPIRED BY THE COMIC STRIP TOON *SHERLOCKO THE MONK!*

Art by Gus Mager, 1910.

This 1999 edition is published by Gramercy Books, a division of Random House Value Publishing, Inc., 201 East 50th Street, New York, New York 10022.

Gramercy Books™ and design are trademarks of Random House Value Publishing, Inc.

Packaged by YOE! Studio™
P.O. Box 559
Peekskill, NY 10566
yoestudi@cloud9.net
YOE! Studio is a division of and trademark of Craig Yoe Studio, Inc.

Random House
New York | Toronto | London | Sydney | Auckland
http://www.randomhouse.com/

Printed and bound in the United States of America

A CIP catalog record for this book is available from the Library of Congress.

Weird but True Toon Factoids/by Craig Yoe
ISBN 0-517-20170-4

8 7 6 5 4 3 2

FOREWARNED!

TOON MUCH

Walt Disney once confessed, "I love Mickey Mouse more than any woman I've ever known."

I feel just like that except I'm not monogamous. Or should I say mouse-ogamous?

One look at Betty Boop makes me want to boop-oop-a-doop. Popeye floats my boat. Krazy Kat drives me...yes, krazy. But, as a grown man I'm truly ashamed of my feelings about teenager Judy Jetson and my dreams of the future we could have together.

I really must rid myself of these unnatural desires. This toon-obsession, as it were.

"Were," because this book has cured me. I've been working on compiling toon factoids for over three decades (weird but true!). Toon after toon. I'm sick of toons. I've got to get a life. Maybe even find a real relationship with a real female, not just some paramour on paper. From now on I'm thru with toons!

Uh...Excuse me, I just heard the evening paper hit my doorstep...gotta go...I wanna see what Mary Worth is up to. You see...I have this thing for older women...

—Craig Yoe.

6

IN-TRUE-DUCTION!

BETMAN

Those of you who think of me as a serious actor must be reminded that Batman is not real. We created our classic movie and TV show from a toon. That is why I've been asked to write these few words.

For those, like myself, who are as emotionally scarred as the creator of these pages is (or at least pretends to be), this book arrives too late. Had we this book in hand years ago, some of us could have won fortunes in toon-trivia wagers.

Imagine being able to challenge your buddy to put up a hundred on something as remote and esoteric as where Bob Kane got his inspiration for The Joker (page 45). Or what great screen beauty has lips like Donald Duck (page 59). Or which cartoonist was knighted (answer on page 46).

Well, possibly it's not too late after all. Just turn the pages and read carefully. Then, get someone to "put up or shut up."

And send Craig Yoe a thank-you note.

P.S. My personal favorite part of the book is page 29. What a profile!

—Adam West,
TV's Batman;
www.adamwest.com.

7

NEW YUK!

The one and only Craig Yoe is a specialist in a curious kind of humor. You too will see it as you go through this book.

He is a master of funny! The old *New Yorker* had this with its great cartoonists that it must find again. Yoe is not a yo-yo—his name just sounds like it!

—Marc Davis,
Animator of Cruella De Vil;
One of Disney's Nine Old Men.

DO BE SILLY

Craig Yoe's wonderful *Weird but True Toon Factoids* is a book about grown adults who sit at home all day drawing silly pictures—and that's not the weird part. Weird but true!

—Patrick McDonnell,
Creator of the comic strip *Mutts*.

TRAIN OF THOUGHT

Even though I'm questionably referred to as the father of Jiminy Cricket, I have yet to tattoo his likeness on any of my body parts. All real crickets look most like fetid cockroaches, but a cricket with a human face?...an entomological disgrace!

Craig Yoe's *Weird but True Toon Factoids* just has to raise eyebrows for some browsers and lower eyebrows for others. However, for me, my eyes are totally crossed. Has Viagra passed me by?

—Ward Kimball,
Creator of Jiminy Cricket;
One of Disney's Nine Old Men.

8

FACE FRONT

Robert Ripley must be smiling down from Toon Heaven right now! Super-heroic Craig Yoe has taken the sensational Rip's Believe It or Not shtick and done a mighty and marvelous job of turning it on the world of comics, cartoons, and their creators—and even on ol' Ripley himself! I never knew how wild, woolly, and weird we creators and our creations were until I read this titanic toon tome! But now I am a

believer. A true believer. Okay, a weird but true believer! 'Nuff said! Or should I say "Believe it!"—or what?!

—Stan Lee,
Co-creator of Spider-Man;
Publisher of Marvel Comics.

Gary A.

YABBA-DABBA CAN-DO

Cartoons have always fascinated me. As a kid, I can remember no greater pleasure than coming home from school to watch cartoons on the local TV station. I waited all week for those wonderful cartoon-filled Saturday mornings. And I waited all year for those glorious Disney movies to be released. Later, I became a devoted fan of comic books and the daily newspaper comic strips. I thought it would be wonderful to someday have a job where I could draw cartoons. When I got to college, one of my classes was an advertising design course. All semester, on every assignment that I turned in, I used cartoons as solutions for my design layouts. Finally, at the end of the course, my professor wrote an exasperated note on the bottom of my last assignment. It read, "You can't always reduce everything to a cartoon!" And then he added, "...well, then again, maybe you can." My feelings exactly, professor.

Craig's book is for all of us who can't get enough of cartoons. It's a little behind-the-scenes look at our favorite medium. It's full of funny stuff that even I didn't know. In short, it's for all those who want to reduce everything to a cartoon. Enjoy.

—Gary Albright,
Vice President of Trade Creative Services,
Cartoon Network.

WEIRD BUT DUE

Sure toons can entertain. No one has got more laughs or thrills from Beetle Bailey or Batman than me. But the hard-working, roll-up-their-sleeves, get-down-to-business, get-off-their-duff toons, like Tony the Tiger, Elsie the Cow, Sonny the Cocoa Puff Bird, and our own little Big Boy rarely get their due.

These no-nonsense toons put people on payrolls...they keep Americans working! Craig Yoe, a working stiff himself (albeit one of the more creative ones) knows this and gives these spokestoons (as he likes to call them) their place in cartoon history. God bless these working toons of the world and God bless Craig Yoe!

—Chris Elias,
Vice Chairman,
Big Boy Restaurants.

IN THE BEGINNING!

CARTOONIST *B. KLIBAN* WAS AFFECTIONATELY
KNOWN TO HIS FRIENDS AS *"HAP,"* HAVING BEEN
BORN ON *NEW YEAR'S DAY!*

GOOD GRIEF!

CHARLES SCHULZ HAS ALWAYS *HATED* THE NAME *PEANUTS!*

Schulz as he sees himself.

"I TAWT I TAW A NAKED TWEETY BIRD!"

...SAID CENSORS WHO THEN *DEMANDED* A CHANGE FROM *TWEETY'S* ORIGINAL *PINK* COLOR TO *YELLOW!*

11

Caruso clowned around with this self-caricature.

celebrity cartoonist dept.

TUNES & TOONS

CARUSO, THE WORLD'S MOST FAMOUS TENOR, WAS ALSO A *TALENTED CARICATURIST* WHO WAS OFFERED A *$50,000 YEARLY SALARY TO DRAW!*

POP ART!

POP STAR *GEORGE MICHAEL* EXPOSES HIS *BIG* CARTOONING TALENT!

"IS THAT A **CARROT** IN YOUR POCKET...?"

DOES *ROGER RABBIT* FIND *JESSICA* EXCITING? "ARE YOU KIDDING?" SAYS *CHARLES FLEISCHER*, *ROGER'S* VOICE. "WHY DO YOU THINK HE WEARS PANTS?! *BUGS BUNNY DOESN'T WEAR PANTS!*"

12

...and at her age, yet!

A WOMB WITH A VIEW!

FATHERED BY A CARTOONIST WHO WENT BY HIS INITIALS, *LAF*, *EGGBERT* WAS THE *WEIRDEST TOON EVER CONCEIVED...* *A TALKING FETUS!*

TWIN TOONS dept.

I YAM WHAT HE IS!

IN 1932, *POPEYE* LOOK-ALIKE *MILTON BLACK* GOT A $250-A-WEEK JOB MAKING APPEARANCES AS THE *SAILOR MAN!*

BOY WONDER !

INCREDIBLY, *PAUL LEVITZ* BECAME THE EDITORIAL COORDINATOR OF THE *MAJORITY* OF THE *DC COMICS* LINE WHILE HE WAS *JUST A TEENAGER!*

Paul, a teen titan, by Dave Manak.

13

MOMMY *WEIRDEST!*

HOMER DAVENPORT'S MOTHER WAS *OBSESSED* THAT HE BECOME THE NEXT *THOMAS NAST.* WHILE PREGNANT, SHE *DEVOURED NAST'S* CARTOONS AND LATER FORCED *HOMER* TO DRAW AT *AGE 3!* BEFORE SHE DIED, SHE *ORDERED* THE BOY'S FATHER TO KEEP HIM DRAWING. HER *WEIRD PLAN* WORKED: *DAVENPORT* BECAME THE *MOST FAMOUS, HIGHEST-PAID CARTOONIST OF HIS TIME!*

Homer does Homer. Doh!

Davenport.

Mommy.

STRIP TEASE!

IN 1930, A FAKE *"SLIP-UP"* WAS CONCOCTED TO LAUNCH THE NEW COMIC STRIP, *BLONDIE.* VIRTUALLY EVERY NEWSPAPER EDITOR IN THE COUNTRY RECEIVED A SUITCASE FULL OF *LINGERIE* TAGGED WITH *BLONDIE'S* NAME, FOLLOWED BY A TELEGRAM APOLOGIZING FOR THE *"MIX-UP"*!

WEIRD BUT WOO-WOO!

This vintage paper doll gives *Weird but True* readers a peek at Blondie's undies.

DO HAVE A COW, MAN!

GOT MONIKER? WHEN SPOKESTOON *ELSIE THE COW* WAS EXPECTING, THE BORDEN MILK COMPANY RECEIVED *4 MILLION SUGGESTIONS* FOR HER OFFSPRINGS' NAMES!

MMM, ELSIE, NICE CALVES!

REJECTION STRIP!

FACT! AFTER YEARS OF BITTER REJECTION FROM COMIC STRIP SYNDICATES, *JERRY SIEGEL* AND *JOE SHUSTER'S SUPERMAN* ARTWORK WAS CUT UP AND REARRANGED FOR THE NEW MEDIUM OF COMIC BOOKS...

THE REST IS HISTORY!

"Army Medical Examiner: 'At last, a perfect soldier!'"

Minor (1884-1952), by fellow Commie cartoonist Art Young.

THE UNGENTLEMANLY ART STATES, "ROBERT MINOR... MIGHT HAVE BEEN THE OUTSTANDING AMERICAN CARTOONIST OF THE TWENTIETH CENTURY IF HE HAD NOT INSTEAD CHOSEN TO BECOME 'FIGHTING BOB,' COMMUNIST PARTY CANDIDATE FOR GOVERNOR OF NEW YORK..."

15

BUD FISHER AS SEEN BY HIMSELF

HORSE CENTS!

IN 1907, *BUD FISHER* DREW THE FIRST SUCCESSFUL DAILY COMIC STRIP, *MUTT AND JEFF*, FOR *$15* PER WEEK. THIS STRIP ABOUT THE RACE TRACK MADE HIM *SO RICH* HE BECAME THE OWNER OF THE *LARGEST STABLE OF THOROUGHBRED HORSES IN AMERICA!*

A CARTOONIST AT THE END OF HIS ROPE!

ROBERT NILSON CREATED A WHOLE BOOK OF CARTOONS ABOUT "HILARIOUS" HANGINGS!

I HATE TO BURST YOUR BUBBLE, BUT...

THE WORLD'S WIDEST READ COMIC STRIP ISN'T *PEANUTS* OR *DILBERT*—IT'S BUBBLE GUM'S *BAZOOKA JOE!* IRONICALLY, JOE'S STRIP IS ALSO THE *WORLD'S TINIEST!*

Yo, Joe! Joe is the original wrapper!

SEDUCTION OF THE INNOCENT dept.

STAND! DRAW NOT YOUR BLOOD IN SIGHT OF THE KILLER HEADS, THEY WILL LIVE!

AYE, FIVE WILL LIVE, BUT ONE SHALL REMAIN SILENT —

LOOK, JANE, LOOK! LOOK! LOOK! LOOK!

IN HIS 1953 BOOK *SEDUCTION OF THE INNOCENT,* PSYCHIATRIST *FREDERIC WERTHAM, M.D.,* REVEALS THE SHOCKING IMAGE HIDDEN IN A COMIC BOOK PANEL, "*...FOR CHILDREN WHO KNOW HOW TO LOOK!*"

BLESSED BE THE TIES!

DICK TRACY CREATOR *CHESTER GOULD* WAS BURIED WITH A *DICK TRACY* CRIME-STOPPER'S *BADGE* AND A HAND-PAINTED *DICK TRACY TIE!*

CHESTER GOULD 1900 1985

Hallo,
Switty Pie!
Affectunetly,
Lena.
And grittings from
Basil Wolverton

A FACE ONLY A *SURREALIST*, A *CROONER*, AND A *CARTOONIST* COULD LOVE!

PRESENTING *LENA THE HYENA*, WINNER OF THE *UGLIEST GIRL IN THE WORLD CONTEST* HELD IN *AL CAPP'S LI'L ABNER* COMIC STRIP. THE *JUDGES* WERE *SALVADOR DALI, FRANK SINATRA,* AND *CAPP.* LENA CAME TO LIFE UNDER THE PEN OF ARTIST *BASIL "BEAN BEAK" WOLVERTON!*

A Wolver-toon of Wolverton.

MS. BOOPADOOP-BUMSTEAD!

BLONDIE'S MAIDEN NAME WAS *BOOPADOOP!*

dept.

MUNSTER CHEESE-CAKE!

THIS FELLOW WITH AN UNUSUAL CELLO IS BY *FRED GWYNNE,* TV'S *HERMAN MUNSTER!*

Gwynne.

Gwynne.

GIVING NEW MEANING TO THE WORD "BEDROCK"

IS BETTY BETTER?

ESQUIRE MAGAZINE REPORTS THAT **58.2%** OF MEN SURVEYED WOULD LOVE TO *"YABBA-DABBA-DO-IT"* WITH *BETTY RUBBLE,* WHILE ONLY 30.4% PREFER *WILMA FLINTSTONE!*

BROWN KNOWS

BUSTER BROWN STARTED AS A MERE COMIC STRIP TOON IN 1902, BUT HE *REALLY* KNEW HOW *TO SELL*... EVERYTHING FROM CLOTHES TO CANDY, GAMES, BREAD, JEWELRY, AND OF COURSE, *BUSTER BROWN SHOES!* *MARY JANE SHOES* ARE NAMED AFTER *BUSTER'S GIRLFRIEND!*

Buster's creator R. F. Outcault, by J. S. Anderson, early 1900s.

Tarpe and her sweet pussycat.

Never before published! An Ub Iwerks' *Steamboat Willie* drawing.

IT'S GOT A GOOD TEAT AND IT'S EASY TO DANCE TO!

ANIMATION HISTORIAN *JOHN CANEMAKER* DESCRIBES HOW *MICKEY,* IN HIS FIRST RELEASED CARTOON *STEAMBOAT WILLIE* (1928), "MADE MUSIC FROM AN *ASTONISHING* ASSORTMENT OF INSTRUMENTS, INCLUDING A CAT'S TAIL, A COW'S TEETH, A GOOSE'S NECK, AND A *PIG'S TEATS!*"

SEX DOESN'T SELL!

IN 1947, *37* NEWSPAPERS CANCELLED *MISS FURY* WHEN *TARPE MILLS* DREW THIS *RACY* PANEL IN THE COMIC *STRIP!*

HE LOOKS MARVEL-OUS!

ELVIS PRESLEY, A *BIG* COMIC BOOK FAN, MODELED HIS *HAIR*, WIDE-LEGGED *POSES*, AND *CAPES* AFTER HIS *FAVORITE* SUPERHERO, *CAPTAIN MARVEL, JR.!*

20

Was this mouse created by the British Disny and Iwrks?

THOSE BLOODY BRITS COULDN'T SPELL BEETLES RIGHT, EITHER!

THIS CUTE LITTLE *CARTOON MOUSE* IN HIS *LITTLE RED SHORTS* IS NAMED *MICKY* (NO "E") *MOUSE.* HE APPEARED IN A *BRITISH* COMIC BOOK NEARLY A *DECADE* BEFORE THE *AMERICAN MICKEY* (WITH AN "E") *MOUSE'S* DEBUT!

TOONVESTITES dept.

HEY THERE, SAILOR!

Popeye in drag by E.C. Segar.

MAE QUESTEL, THE VOICE OF OLIVE OYL, DID POPEYE FOR 6 OR 7 CARTOONS WHILE JACK MERCER WAS OVERSEAS DURING WORLD WAR II! "I CAN STILL DO THE VOICE," MUMBLED MAE! I YAM WHAT I AIN'T!

Jack Mercer by Chuck Thorndike.

Questel also did the voice of Betty Boop.

QUIRKY QUOTES dept.

OH! OH! OH! MAGOO! ...YOU'VE DONE IT AGAIN!

JIM BACKUS, THE VOICE OF MR. MAGOO, SAID, "THE ONLY THING LEFT TO DO IS AN X-RATED MAGOO!"

21

MONKEY SEE, MONKEY DO!

THE PURPLE APE ON THIS MAY 1951 COMIC BOOK JUMPED THE SALES SO MUCH THAT ALL THE DC COMICS EDITORS WANTED TO APE IT BY PUTTING PURPLE APES ON THEIR COVERS. THE PUBLISHER WAS FORCED TO LEASH THE EDITORS IN WITH A MONTHLY PURPLE APE LIMIT!

Monkey business by artist Win Mortimer.

NAME THAT TOON dept.

TRIPLE BILL

DONALD DUCK'S NEPHEWS *HUEY, DEWEY,* AND *LOUIE* WERE NAMED AFTER POLITICIANS *THOMAS DEWEY* AND *HUEY LONG,* AND *DISNEY* EMPLOYEE *LOUIE SCHMITT!*

An unpublished comic book cover by Carl Barks.

WHO'S THE REAL POOP?

JOHN K., CREATOR OF *REN* AND *STIMPY,* CLAIMS *SOUTH PARK* RIPPED OFF *MR. HANKEY THE CHRISTMAS POO* FROM *NUTTY THE FRIENDLY DUMP. TREY PARKER* AND *MATT STONE* COUNTER *MR. HANKEY* WAS INDEPENDENTLY CONCEIVED. *WEIRD BUT #2!*

Nutty and Mr. Hankey.

22

TOONVESTITES dept.

LITTLE "ANDROGYNOUS" ANNIE!

THIS TOON WAS CONCEIVED BY *HAROLD GRAY* (1864-1968) TO BE A YOUNG BOY NAMED *OTTO. CAPTAIN JOSEPH PATTERSON,* PUBLISHER OF THE *NEW YORK DAILY NEWS,* PROCLAIMED, *"THE KID LOOKS LIKE A PANSY. JUST PUT A SKIRT ON HIM AND WE'LL CALL HIM LITTLE ORPHAN ANNIE!"*

Harold Gray by Ernie Bushmiller.

Oh, YES, INDEEDY... ISN'T THIS FOHTUNATE? WHY, IT'S JUST THE THING!

9-21-44

...BUT HOW DOES MARGE FEEL ABOUT **CRULLERS?**

FAMED PSYCHOTHERAPIST *DR. WILL MILLER'S* ANALYSIS OF *HOMER SIMPSON'S* ATTRACTION TO DONUTS: "WHEN *HOMER* SAYS 'MMMM' TO A DONUT, *HE'S REALLY SAYING 'MMMM' TO SEX!*"

Homer-erotic.

NAME THAT TOON dept.

I SEE.... MY NAME IS DURAND, BUT DON'T ASK ME HOW TO SPELL IT. I LEFT EARTH OVER HALF A CENTURY AGO.

I THINK MY NAME IS BARBARELLA!

23

THEY WERE *FONDA* BARBARELLA!

ROCK BAND *DURAN DURAN'S* NAME WAS INSPIRED BY A CHARACTER FROM THE FRENCH COMIC BOOK STARRING *BARBARELLA*, WHICH WAS ALSO THE SOURCE OF THE *JANE FONDA* MOVIE!

TURN ON, TOON IN,...

WHEN *DISNEY'S* 1940 HALLUCINOGENIC MASTERPIECE *FANTASIA* WAS RE-RELEASED IN THE *PSYCHEDELIC SIXTIES*, ANIMATOR *ART BABBITT* WAS ASKED BY SOME *HIPPIES* WHETHER HE WAS *ON DRUGS* WHILE MAKING THE FILM. *"YES, I WAS ON DRUGS,"* QUIPPED *BABBITT*, *"EX-LAX* AND *PEPTO BISMOL!"*

The far-out sixties *Fantasia* poster.

HELLO, DOLLY!

JACKIE ORMES, CREATOR OF THE *TORCHY BROWN* COMIC STRIP, ALSO CREATED THE *VERY FIRST COMMERCIAL BLACK DOLL!*

Jackie O.

MEET THE WINSTONES!

AS AN EARLY SPONSOR OF *THE FLINTSTONES*, *WINSTON* CIGARETTES WERE HAWKED BY *FRED*, *WILMA*, AND *BARNEY* IN COMMERCIALS. *FRED* EVEN SANG THE *WINSTON'S* THEME SONG! *YABBA-DABBA DUMB!*

WHAT A RIP!

IN PURSUIT OF *WEIRD FACTOIDS* FOR HIS *RIPLEY'S BELIEVE IT OR NOT* NEWSPAPER FEATURE, CARTOONIST *ROBERT RIPLEY* TRAVELED TO *197 COUNTRIES*...MORE THAN *ANY OTHER PERSON!*

LINDBERGH WAS THE 67th MAN TO MAKE A NON-STOP FLIGHT OVER THE ATLANTIC OCEAN!

Robert Ripley's most famous statement shocked a nation! But, Lindbergh's was the first solo flight!

WITH THE WEALTH FROM THE EMPIRE HE CREATED, *RIPLEY* BUILT A *HUGE MANSION*, AND KEPT A COLLECTION OF *SHRUNKEN HEADS, BACKWARD-SWIMMING FISH*, AND A PRIVATE *HAREM* OF *WOMEN* COLLECTED FROM THE *FOUR CORNERS OF THE WORLD! BELIEVE IT OR NOT!*

25

ANTI-CARTOON BILL

Homer Davenport, by Grant Wright, circa 1904.

THEY COULDN'T TAKE A JOKE!

HOMER DAVENPORT'S SCATHING POLITICAL CARTOONS SO *ANGERED THOMAS PLATT* (RIGHT), THAT IN 1897, HE TRIED TO INTRODUCE AN *ANTI-CARTOON LAW* IN *NEW YORK STATE!*

Davenport compared Platt to "Boss" Tweed in this drawing, "They Never Liked Cartoons."

MMM! SEE YOU IN THE FUNNIES!

MAUREEN O'SULLIVAN, WHO PLAYED *JANE* IN THE *TARZAN* MOVIES, DRESSED IN *TARZAN* COMIC STRIP PAGES!

A boost to Tarzan's circulation for sure!

★celebrity★ cartoonist dept.
TOONS, ANYONE?
...ASKS *W.C. FIELDS!*

WORLD WAR TOONR dept.

BUMS AWAY!

STRIP TOON *JANE* STRIPPED IN THE (LONDON) *DAILY MIRROR!* THE U.S. ARMY NEWSPAPER *ROUND-UP* REPORTED: "WELL, SIRS, YOU CAN GO HOME NOW...*JANE PEELED* A WEEK AGO. THE BRITISH 37TH DIVISION *IMMEDIATELY* GAINED *6 MILES* AND THE BRITISH *ATTACKED* IN THE ARAKAN. MAYBE WE AMERICANS *OUGHT TO HAVE JANE, TOO!*"

From the famous sequence in 1943.

THE ARTIST FORMALLY KNOWN FOR PRINCE!

ABOUT HIS FIRST JOB, *HAROLD (PRINCE VALIANT) FOSTER* SAID, "I GOT $17.50 A WEEK FOR DRAWING *LADIES' UNDERWEAR.* I PUT MY *WHOLE SOUL* INTO IT!"

TOO LONG HAVE YOU MADE ME A HERO, FOSTER, NOW WRITE SOME PLEASANT SIN INTO MY SAGA

Foster and his foster children.

27

CHARLIE HORSE!

CHARLES SCHULZ'S LIFELONG NICKNAME IS *SPARKY,* AFTER *BARNEY GOOGLE'S* GOOD OL' HORSE, *SPARK PLUG!*

Spark Plug's DeBeck as he saw himself.

ONE FROM THE **FUNNY** FARM!

A *MENTAL HOSPITAL* IN LINCOLN, ILL., USED THIS *CHARLES ADDAMS* CARTOON TO TEST THE *MENTAL CAPACITY* OF ITS PATIENTS! SOME OF THE PATIENTS SAW *NOTHING WRONG WITH IT!*

FLYBOY!

MIGHTY MOUSE WAS ORIGINALLY CONCEIVED TO BE A *MIGHTY FLY!*

UDDER NONSENSE!

NO ONE UNDERSTOOD THIS *FAR SIDE* CARTOON, NOT EVEN CREATOR *GARY LARSON'S MOTHER!* EVEN *GARY* WAS CONFUSED, ADMITTING, *"IT OBVIOUSLY DID NOT WORK AS I INTENDED"!*

Cow tools.

HOLY ARTISTIC LICENSE!

ADAM WEST PENNED THIS *SELF-PORTRAIT* FOR *WEIRD BUT TRUE!*

HOORAY FOR HOLLYROCK!

COUNTLESS GUEST CELEBS HAVE POPPED UP ON *THE FLINTSTONES,* INCLUDING *PERRY MASONRY, ED SULLYSTONE, STONEY CURTIS,* AND *ANN-MARGROCK!* "...ALL THESE YEARS LATER THESE LITTLE KIDS ASK ME IF I'M *ANN-MARGROCK!*" CHUCKLED *ANN-MARGRET!*

29

SEEING RED

RUDOLPH THE RED-NOSED REINDEER STARTED *NOT* AS A *SONG* OR EVEN AS A *TV MOVIE,* BUT WAS FIRST INTRODUCED TO THE PUBLIC IN A 1951 *COMIC BOOK!*

An unpublished sketch for the Golden Books video cover by Luke McDonnell.

"That reminds me. Have you seen the new show at the Folies Bergères?"

WORLD WAR TOONR dept.

NAZI ANSWER THEY WANTED!

IN *WW II*, NAZIS REPEATEDLY TRIED TO TEMPT PRISONER *JEAN BELLUS*, CREATOR OF *CLEMENTINE CHERIE*, WITH *FREEDOM* IF HE WOULD DRAW FOR THEIR FRENCH *COLLABORATIONIST PAPERS*. HE TOLD THEM TO *GO SCRATCH!*

Kane pictured himself in his infancy.

The Penguin will go down in infamy!

WOOFIN' WHILE YOU WORK!

CHARLES SCHULZ WAS *SHOCKED* TO LEARN THAT *SNOOPY* WAS CONSIDERED AS A NAME FOR ONE OF *WALT DISNEY'S SEVEN DWARFS!*

SMOKIN'!

INSPIRED BY THIS *CIGARETTE-TOTING PENGUIN*, ARTIST *BOB KANE* CREATED HIS FAMOUS *BATMAN VILLAIN!*

The Lizard King.

The Comix King.

TO CRAIG — R. CRUMB ANGOLÉME, 1992

A previously unpublished drawing of Mr. Natural and Flakey Floont, 1971.

31

C'MON, BABY, LIGHT MY FUNNIES!

JIM MORRISON, LEGENDARY LEADER OF *THE DOORS*, SAID IN A 1970 INTERVIEW, "WHEN I READ OR WATCH TV OR SEE MOVIES, I HARDLY EVER CRACK UP...LIKE REALLY ROLL ON THE FLOOR...BUT *ZAP COMIX* MAKES IT. *CRUMB* IS, I THINK, ONE OF THE MOST...*BRILLIANT GENIUSES* TO COME AROUND IN A LONG TIME. EVER SINCE I'VE BEEN READING *ZAP*, I SEE THE WORLD AS A *ZAP COMIX!*"

Mutt and Jeff standing by their man, Bud.

MOOLA & OOH-LA-LA!

LI'L ABNER'S CREATOR, *AL CAPP,* ON WHY HE CHOSE A CAREER IN CARTOONING: "I HEARD *BUD (MUTT AND JEFF) FISHER* GOT *$3,000 A WEEK* AND WAS CONSTANTLY MARRYING *FRENCH COUNTESSES!*"

Al Capp

Li'l Abner and his best bud, Al.

32

LOVE ME T-T-TENDER...

PORKY PIG, DAFFY DUCK, FOGHORN LEGHORN, AND OTHER *WARNER BROS.* CELEBRITY TOONS CUT AN ALBUM OF *ELVIS PRESLEY'S* GREATEST HITS!

BLEEP BLEEP!

"IT'S *FRIGHTENING.* I WATCHED A *ROAD RUNNER* CARTOON WITH MY LITTLE GIRL. THEY DROPPED A ROCK ON THE COYOTE AND FLATTENED HIM, BUT HE POPPED RIGHT UP AGAIN. THAT'S REALLY *SHOCKING* TO ME BECAUSE WHEN A CHILD GROWS UP WITH THAT SORT OF THING, HE'LL FEEL HE CAN GO AROUND *HITTING PEOPLE ON THE HEAD* WITH A *HAMMER* AND THEY'LL *BE ALL RIGHT!*" —CHARLES *(DEATH WISH)* BRONSON.

LET THE FUR FLY!

TOM AND JERRY WERE FIRST CONCEIVED BY *HANNA* AND *BARBERA* TO BE A *DOG* AND *FOX!*

A HULK OF A DIFFERENT COLOR!

THE INDELIBLE HULK? NAH..."OL' GREEN SKIN" WAS ORIGINALLY *GRAY!* THE COLOR GAVE THE PRINTER *PROBLEMS,* SO HE WAS *CHANGED* TO HIS NOW FAMILIAR *EMERALD* SHADE! *WEIRD BUT HUE!*

33

It's not easy being green. The gray Hulk in his May 1962 debut.

ANOTHER CASE OF NOT MINDING YOUR PEAS AND HUES!

Pea superman, 1960.

The fur-covered, flesh-colored original, 1927.

LIKE *THE HULK,* ANOTHER *GIANT TOON* WASN'T ORIGINALLY *GREEN—* THE GREEN GIANT!

Muffaroo warns Lovekins not to go near the water.

But she does go and alarms a nice lady.

By falling off the embankment.

Old man Muffaroo brings a boat.

And throws it to Little Lady Lovekins.

The boat strikes the water with a splash,

WHAT'S UP, *DOC?*

THE INCREDIBLE UPSIDE-DOWNS, CREATED IN 1903, ARE FIRST READ *RIGHT-SIDE UP,* THEN FINISHED BY READING *UPSIDE DOWN!* *GUSTAVE VERBEEK* ACCOMPLISHED THIS FOR *65 INSTALLMENTS!* ¡WEIRD BUT TOPSY-TURVY!

A 1952 self-caricature of the blushing artist.

KREMOS OF THE KROP!

A TOON HISTORIAN TOUTED *KREMOS* AS "THE *NUMERO UNO* DELINEATOR OF *DELECTABLE DAMSELS*." BUT THE CARTOONIST WAS SAID TO BE *SHY* AROUND WOMEN, *BLUSHING* AT THEIR *MERE GLANCE!*

35

"Before and After," 1920's self-caricatures by Sidney Smith.

An unpublished drawing of Andy... and his alleged inspiration.

TOOTH & CONSEQUENCES!

SIDNEY SMITH'S ANDY GUMP WAS ALLEGEDLY BASED ON REAL-LIFE *ANDY WHEAT* WHO, AFTER A *TOOTH EXTRACTION*, GOT SUCH A BAD INFECTION HIS *LOWER JAW* HAD TO BE *REMOVED!*

MOLE REMOVAL

WHEN *THE MOLE* FROM *DICK TRACY* DIED, FANS STAGED A *MOCK FUNERAL!*

"LET NO MAN WRITE MY EPITAPH"

...COULD HAVE BEEN THE MOTTO OF CARICATURIST *RALPH BARTON* WHO WROTE HIS OWN OBITUARY... *THEN TOOK HIS OWN LIFE!*

A drawing from life.

RALPH BARTON

Baer by Bart, his cartooning teacher...

... and the real Baer.

RUNNING BAER

PRIOR TO HIS ELECTION TO CONGRESS IN 1917, *JOHN BAER* WAS A CARTOONIST. HE RAN ON A PLATFORM PROMISING TO *REQUIRE* NEWSPAPER EDITORS *TO RUN CARTOONS ON THE FRONT PAGE!*

SPECIAL DELIVERY

THE FAMILY CIRCUS CREATOR *BIL KEANE* DONNED A *SURGICAL MASK* THE DAY HE "CONCEIVED" *BABY PJ.* HE AND HIS WIFE CONCEIVED THEIR FIVE CHILDREN, BUT *KEANE* CLAIMS, "I CREATED *THIS* ONE MYSELF...ON PAPER. *NOTHING TO IT!"*

GET THE LEAD OUT!

FACT! BROADWAY CARICATURIST *AL HIRSCHFELD* DRAWS HIS SUBJECTS *IN THE DARK, IN HIS POCKET,* ON A PAD WITH A LITTLE *PENCIL STUB!* *WEIRD BUT TOO MUCH!*

FORE!" WEIRD BUT TRUE"

IRON MAN!

ACCORDING TO GOLF LEGEND *GARY PLAYER,* "THE IDEAL BUILD FOR A GOLFER WOULD BE STRONG HANDS, BIG FOREARMS, THIN NECK, AND A FLAT CHEST. *HE'D LOOK LIKE POPEYE!*"

37

Da Vinci.

Kane.

WINGING IT!

DID DA VINCI PROPHESY BATMAN?
DID BOB KANE "BAT CHANNEL" DA VINCI?
BOB KANE ADMITS THAT *LEONARDO DA VINCI'S FLYING MACHINE* INFLUENCED HIS DESIGN FOR THE *CAPED CRUSADER!*
WEIRD BAT TRUE!

Herriman by Chuck Thorndike.

(AH-LiL AINJIL)

PUNG

ZIP

HAVE AT YOU, KAT

- KAT... 'WAS WUNDER. - THINE IN THE GLORY GEO HERRIMAN
L.A. EVENING HERALD · 1922

A rare unpublished 1922 drawing.

BESIDES BEING KRAZY...

GEORGE HERRIMAN SOMETIMES REFERRED TO *KRAZY KAT* AS A *MALE*, SOMETIMES AS A *FEMALE!*

THEY PUT HIM ON THE MAP!

SQUIRREL GULCH, COLO., WAS RENAMED *STEVE CANYON* IN HONOR OF THE CHARACTER CREATED BY *MILTON CANIFF!*

STEVE CANYON for HAROLD SHELL — Best Wishes, MILTON CANIFF NY · 22 OCT, 1947

An unpublished sketch from 1947, the strip's first year.

38

THE HONEYMOON WAS ALMOST OVER!

ASKED IF *THE HONEYMOONERS* INFLUENCED THE CREATION OF *THE FLINTSTONES,* BILL HANNA SAID, "*JACKIE GLEASON* WAS GOING TO *SUE,* BUT WAS *TALKED OUT OF IT* BY HIS *LAWYERS!*"

Frost by Thomas Eakins, circa 1886.

An unpublished variation, circa 1890, from Frost's famous *Bull Calf and Other Tales*.

FROST *DOESN'T* BITE!

JOSEPH PENNELL SAID OF *A. B. FROST'S* CARTOONS, "TO COMPARE THEM WITH THE DRIVEL...IN EVERY NEWSPAPER IN THE LAND IS TO NOTE HOW THIS COUNTRY HAS *DEGENERATED...FROST* IS THE *ONLY* COMIC ARTIST WE HAVE...THE REST ARE MOSTLY A *DISGRACE*, EVEN TO THIS LAND OF *ARTLESS, CHILDISH VULGARIANS!*"

39

CHRISTMAS POTTY!

THE SCATOLOGICALLY DRIVEN CARTOON *SOUTH PARK* STARTED AS A JOKE "CHRISTMAS CARD" VIDEO CIRCULATED AMONG *HOLLYWOOD INSIDERS.* *GEORGE CLOONEY* (WHO WAS THE VOICE OF *SPARKY, THE GAY DOG,* IN A LATER EPISODE) PIRATED *100 COPIES* TO SHOW TO HIS *100 CLOSEST FRIENDS!*

SPRECHEN SIE QUACK?

CLARENCE NASH, THE VOICE OF *DONALD DUCK*, DESCRIBED DUBBING IN FOREIGN LANGUAGES: "WORDS WERE WRITTEN OUT FOR ME PHONETICALLY. I LEARNED TO *QUACK* IN *FRENCH, SPANISH, PORTUGUESE, JAPANESE, CHINESE*, AND *GERMAN!*"

celebrity cartoonist dept.

DRAWN AT WARP SPEED!

GEORGE TAKEI (STAR TREK'S MR. SULU) PENNED THIS SELF-PORTRAIT ESPECIALLY FOR *WEIRD BUT TRUE!*

40

WHERE'S THE CHURCH? WHERE'S THE STEEPLE?

THIS IS AN 1881 VISION OF *MANHATTAN'S* FUTURE SKYLINE DRAWN BY *THOMAS NAST.* IT SHOWS *TRINITY CHURCH*, THEN THE HIGHEST POINT IN THE CITY, ENGULFED BY TOWERING BUILDINGS. *HIS PREDICTION HAS COME EERILY TRUE!*

4 WARNED IS 4 ARMED!

Holman.

"1506 NIX NIX" OFTEN APPEARED IN *BILL HOLMAN'S SMOKEY STOVER* STRIP TO *WARN* WOMEN TO *STAY AWAY* FROM CARTOONIST *AL POSEN'S APARTMENT!*

Posen by
Chuck Thorndike.

GOD IS MY CO-TOONIST!

BROTHER JUSTIN McCARTHY, A FRANCISCAN *MONK,* WAS THE CARTOONIST OF THE COMIC PANEL *BROTHER JUNIPER!*

41

SOMETHING'S FISHY!

A STORE IN *ARIZONA* SOLD *THE LITTLE MERMAID* VIDEO WRAPPED IN *PLAIN BROWN PAPER!* A WOMAN HAD COMPLAINED THAT THE COVER SHOWED AN *UNMENTIONABLE* PART OF THE *MALE ANATOMY* IN *KING TRITON'S CASTLE!*

ON HIS TROLLEY

FONTAINE FOX (1884-1964) GOT THE IDEA FOR HIS POPULAR *TOONERVILLE TROLLEY* COMIC PANEL WHEN HE TOOK A RIDE IN PELHAM, N.Y., ON A *REAL WACKY TROLLEY!*

F.Fox

IT'S A WONDERFUL LAFF!

THIS IS HOW *JIMMY STEWART* SAW HIS CO-STAR, *HARVEY!*

James Stewart

Felix and a self-portrait by Joe Oriolo.

HYA CRAIG!

JOE ORIOLO 11/5/82

Regards from Felix the Cat

WHAT'S THE FREQUENCY, FELIX?

RCA ENGINEERS TESTED THE *TRANSMISSIONS* OF A *TELEVISION SIGNAL* IN 1928. THEY DAILY TRAINED THEIR *CAMERAS* ON A *FELIX THE CAT* DOLL, MAKING HIM *TV'S FIRST REGULAR STAR!*

IT'S NOT THE **MEAT**, IT'S THE **MOTION PICTURE!**

A FAXED EXCHANGE BETWEEN RIVAL MOVIE PRODUCERS *DON (DAYS OF THUNDER) SIMPSON* AND *JEFF (DICK TRACY) KATZENBERG:* *SIMPSON* BOASTED TO *KATZENBERG,* "WHEREVER YOU GO, YOU WON'T ESCAPE THE *THUNDER!*" *KATZENBERG* RETORTED, "*WAIT 'TIL YOU SEE HOW BIG MY DICK IS!*"

Jeffrey Katzenberg, Hollywood Biggie.

ANIMANIAC!

THE WORLD'S *LARGEST* COLLECTION OF *CARTOON CELS* BELONGS TO MOVIE DIRECTOR *STEVEN SPIELBERG!*

Spielberg by Hirschfeld. (with 3 "Ninas").

43

YEAH, BUT COULD HE LEAP TALL BUILDINGS IN A SINGLE BOUND?!

LITTLE NEMO'S WINSOR McCAY SHARED STAGES WITH *HOUDINI* AND *W.C. FIELDS! McCAY* AMAZED AUDIENCES, DRAWING *FASTER THAN A SPEEDING BULLET... 25 DRAWINGS* IN *15 MINUTES!*

A rare photo of McCay doing his chalk-talk.

celebrity cartoonist dept.

Lennon in the Big Apple.

Lennon in the land of Apple Bonkers.

YOKO

John Lennon 80

44

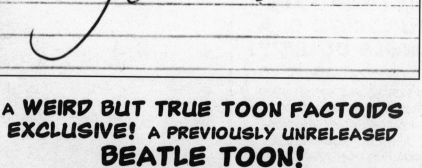

A WEIRD BUT TRUE TOON FACTOIDS EXCLUSIVE! A PREVIOUSLY UNRELEASED BEATLE TOON!

THIS *EXCLUSIVE WEIRD BUT TRUE* CARTOON BY *JOHN LENNON* OF HIMSELF, *YOKO,* AND *SEAN* HAS *NEVER BEFORE APPEARED IN PRINT!*

TWIN TOONS dept.

NO JOKE!

BOB KANE CLAIMS THAT ACTOR CONRAD VEIDT'S APPEARANCE IN A 1928 SILENT FILM INSPIRED THE CREATION OF THE JOKER!

From *Disney Animation: The Illusion of Life*, "Walt's most typical expression caught by one of the staff who preferred to remain anonymous."

UB IWERKS

A rare unpublished self-caricature of Ub Iwerks in his post-Mouse, Flip the Frog days.

Art by George Corley, from 1931. Note Mickey's whiskers and 5 fingers. Gross!

45

CITY MOUSE!

THE PUBLIC WAS CRAZED ABOUT MICKEY MOUSE CREATED BY WALT DISNEY AND UB IWERKS! CHARLIE CHAPLIN TRIED TO CAPITALIZE ON MOUSE MANIA WHEN HE INSISTED THEATER OWNERS OPEN HIS MOVIE CITY LIGHTS (1931) WITH A MICKEY MOUSE CARTOON!

THIS MOUSE PROVIDES ONE GAZILLION PERCENT OF THE RECOMMENDED DAILY ALLOWANCE OF VITAMIN C!

AS PART OF THEIR ANNUAL CITRUS CROP FESTIVAL, THE CITIZENS OF MENTON, FRANCE BUILT THIS *LARGER-THAN-LIFE* REPLICA OF *MICKEY* ENTIRELY OUT OF *LEMONS* AND *ORANGES!*

WEIRD BUT TRUE!

Tenniel as he saw himself.

OH, WHAT A KNIGHT!

POLITICAL CARTOONIST *JOHN TENNIEL,* WHO ILLUSTRATED *LEWIS CARROLL'S ALICE IN WONDERLAND,* WAS *KNIGHTED* IN 1899 FOR *HIS ARTISTIC ACCOMPLISHMENTS!*

SVENGALI CARTOONIST!

CHARLES DANA GIBSON, WHOSE TOONS APPEARED IN *LIFE MAGAZINE* IN THE 1890'S, *ENTRANCED* WOMEN WITH HIS DRAWINGS! WOMEN BECAME *OBSESSED* WITH LOOKING LIKE HIS ARTWORK AND WERE KNOWN AS *GIBSON GIRLS!*

Gibson by J. M. Flagg.

HONEYMOON WOODY

WALTER LANTZ OFTEN CLAIMED THE IDEA FOR *WOODY WOODPECKER* CAME WHEN A PESKY *WOODPECKER* REPEATEDLY INTERRUPTED HIS *HONEYMOON NUPTIALS!*

A really big Woody.

47

BUCK TO THE FUTURE!

BOMBSHELL! THE *"ATOM BOMB"* APPEARED IN THE FIRST SCIENCE FICTION COMIC STRIP, *BUCK ROGERS,* BEFORE IT WAS *EVEN INVENTED!* *WEIRD BUCK TRUE!*

Artwork by Frank Frazetta, *Buck Rogers* comic book cover artist.

DUH!

Hamlin.

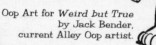

ALLEY OOP CREATOR **VINCENT HAMLIN** EXCLAIMED, "I FOUND IT EXPEDIENT TO KEEP MY HERO'S **INTELLIGENCE QUOTIENT** SOMEWHAT **INFERIOR** TO MY OWN **LIMITED MENTAL MACHINERY**. I NEVER COULD UNDERSTAND HOW A CARTOONIST COULD LIVE WITH A CHARACTER INHERENTLY **SMARTER** THAN **HE** WAS!"

Oop Art for *Weird but True* by Jack Bender, current Alley Oop artist.

"M-I-C...F-D-R..."

PRESIDENT **FRANKLIN DELANO ROOSEVELT** INSISTED THAT A **MICKEY MOUSE** CARTOON BE SHOWN BEFORE **EVERY** MOVIE HE SAW!

48

Everyone's favorite director, the Wood man.

Amazing Grace, how sweet the sound...

PICK A 'PECKER!

WALTER LANTZ REFUSED TO ALLOW WIFE **GRACE** TO AUDITION FOR THE VOICE OF **WOODY WOODPECKER**. SHE SUBMITTED AN **ANONYMOUS** TAPE AND WAS **CHOSEN**, OUT OF **7 OTHER** HOPEFULS, *FOR THE JOB!* HA-HA-HA-**HA**-HA!

Philipon drew a cartoon like this in court
for his own defense.

NICE PEAR!

IN THE 1830'S, CARICATURIST *CHARLES PHILIPON* WAS THROWN INTO PRISON FOR DRAWING *KING LOUIS-PHILIPPE* AS A *PEAR!*

DYNAMIC DUO!

WHEN FITTED FOR HER *SKIN-TIGHT* PURPLE COSTUME, *BATGIRL* TV ACTRESS *YVONNE CRAIG* FOUND "IT *ABSOLUTELY FLATTENED*" HER CHEST. SHE TOLD THE PRODUCER WHO *BERATED* THE COSTUMER FOR RUINING *"TWO OF THE REASONS WE HIRED YVONNE!"* THE COSTUMER REWORKED THE OUTFIT TO BETTER SHOW OFF *YVONNE'S BAT-BUST!*

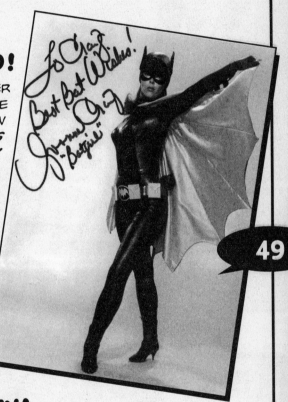

49

OF MICE AND MEN!

EEK AND MEEK ARE *BIZARRE* COMIC STRIP TOONS THAT *EVOLVED* FROM *RODENTS* TO HUMANS! *WEIRD BUT TRUE!*

1965

1969

1977

1982

Autentico fumetto di sigaro. Il migliore del mondo!

Balooneytoon:
Italian master
cartoonist Benito Jacovitti

SMOKE GETS IN YOUR MOUTH!

THE ITALIAN WORD FOR *"COMICS"* IS *"FUMETTI,"* DERIVED FROM *"FUMO,"* THE WORD FOR *"SMOKE"*...BECAUSE THAT'S WHAT ***WORD BALLOONS*** RESEMBLE!

POLLY WANTS A CENSOR!

CLIFF (POLLY AND HER PALS) STERRETT ON EARLY COMIC STRIPS: "YOU HAVE NO IDEA OF THE STRICT *CENSORSHIP* WE WERE FORCED TO WORK UNDER...WE COULDN'T SHOW A *GIRL'S LEG* ABOVE HER SHOE...A *COMIC STRIP KISS* WAS UNHEARD-OF, AND ALL ACTION HAD TO...BE COMPLETED *BEFORE NINE O'CLOCK!"*

50

Cubist cartoonist Cliff Sterrett's self-portrait.

TOP TOON!

THE SONG *"I'M POPEYE THE SAILOR MAN"* WAS ELECTED TO THE *SONGWRITER'S HALL OF FAME! WEIRD BUT TOOT-TOOT!*

A rare photo of McCay on stage, and a Gertie drawing from the original art.

PRE-HYSTERICAL!

IN *1914*, *WINSOR McCAY* CREATED THE *FIRST* COMMERCIALLY SUCCESSFUL ANIMATED CARTOON IN HISTORY. IT REQUIRED *10,000 DRAWINGS* OF ITS STAR, *GERTIE THE DINOSAUR* ...ALL DONE BY *McCAY!*

51

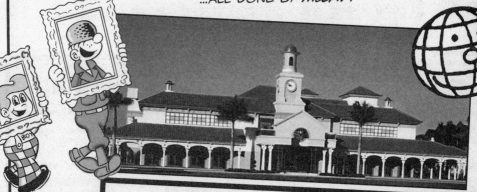

Big Boy visited the museum in a special issue of his comic.

SEE 'UM IN THE MUSEUM!

THE INTERNATIONAL MUSEUM OF CARTOON ART IS IN BOCA RATON, FLA. ITS FOUNDER, *MORT (BEETLE BAILEY) WALKER*, PROCLAIMS THEY HAVE *160,000 CARTOONS!*

52

CARTOONISTS PREFER BLONDES!

SHE MET HIM AT A PARTY WHEN SHE WAS STILL *NORMA JEAN. MARILYN MONROE* LATER SPENT THE DAY AT THE BEACH WITH *BATMAN'S* CREATOR *BOB KANE* AND POSED FOR THE ABOVE SKETCHES!

Groening by Clizia for Weird but True.

HE DOES A HELL OF A JOB!

THE SIMPSONS' MATT GROENING PENS A WEEKLY STRIP, *LIFE IN HELL,* FOR ALTERNATIVE NEWSPAPERS. *GROENING* DECLARES, "IF I CAN MAKE SOMEBODY *LAUGH* AND REALLY *ANNOY THE HELL* OUT OF SOMEBODY ELSE, I THINK I'VE *DONE MY JOB!"*

 **WORLD WAR TOONR** dept.

MOUSE-OLINI!

DURING WWII, *MUSSOLINI* BANNED *ALL* AMERICAN COMIC STRIPS BUT ONE...*HIS BELOVED MICKEY MOUSE!*

Benito, by Kimon Marengo, 1936.

LUPA CAPITOLINA

IN A BEDROOM DARKLY

BY T.F. LEE

53

CARTOONISTS
DO IT IN THE DARK!

EVERY SINGLE CARTOON IN THIS *SWINGIN' SIXTIES* BOOK IS A *BLACK RECTANGLE* WITH A RACY CAPTION ABOUT *HANKY-PANKY* IN *BEDROOMS* WITH THE *LIGHTS TURNED OUT!*

LAZY ARTIST? GENIUS? PERVERT? YOU DECIDE!

"That's a funny place to be ticklish."

"Wake me up when it's over."

Brooks.

Crepax and his Valentina.

HAIR APPARENT!

GUIDO CREPAX'S SEXY TOON *VALENTINA* SPORTS A HAIRCUT INSPIRED BY SILENT FILM SIREN *LOUISE BROOKS!* *WEIRD BUT "DO"!*

LULU IS NOTHING TO SNEEZE AT!

MARGE PLANNED TO HAVE *LITTLE LULU* BE A SPOKESTOON FOR *KLEENEX.* THIS *RILED SATURDAY EVENING POST* EDITORS, WHO *BANNED* THE CARTOON FROM THEIR MAGAZINE! BUT *LULU* RETURNED TO THOSE SAME PAGES IN THE *KLEENEX ADS!* *WEIRD BUT ACHOO!*

54

An unpublished drawing by Marge. Wave to the nice readers, Lulu!

Never before published! A self-caricature by Rube Goldberg.

DAFFYNITION!

RUBE GOLDBERG'S WACKY INVENTIONS HAVE MADE HIS NAME AN *ADJECTIVE* IN THE *DICTIONARY!*

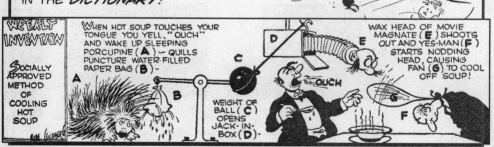

WEEKLY INVENTION

SOCIALLY APPROVED METHOD OF COOLING HOT SOUP

WHEN HOT SOUP TOUCHES YOUR TONGUE YOU YELL, "OUCH" AND WAKE UP SLEEPING PORCUPINE (**A**) — QUILLS PUNCTURE WATER-FILLED PAPER BAG (**B**) —

WEIGHT OF BALL (**C**) OPENS JACK-IN-BOX (**D**) —

WAX HEAD OF MOVIE MAGNATE (**E**) SHOOTS OUT AND YES-MAN (**F**) STARTS NODDING HEAD, CAUSING FAN (**G**) TO COOL OFF SOUP!

OUCH

I AM TONY, HEAR ME ROAR!

IN *TONY THE TIGER'S* EARLIEST INCARNATION, HE CRAWLED ON *ALL FOURS!* HIS *WIFE* AND *KIDS*, WHO USED TO APPEAR IN HIS COMMERCIALS, HAVE *ALL MYSTERIOUSLY DISAPPEARED!* GRRRRRREAT!

POPEYE THE STATUE MAN!

CRYSTAL CITY, TEX., THE *SPINACH* CAPITOL OF THE WORLD, ERECTED A STATUE IN 1937 TO HONOR *POPEYE* AND HIS CREATOR, *E.C. SEGAR,* FOR THEIR INFLUENCE ON AMERICA'S *EATING HABITS!*

CRYSTAL CITY TEX.

POPEYE
ERECTED
MARCH 26 1937
COURTESY
E. C. SEGAR.

AHOY, JACK! AHOY, CHARLIE! I YAM PERFECKLY CONTENTIPATED !!

SPINACH

21 CLUB

Sincerely —

YOURS TO THE LAST ASH!

SEGAR

A rare Popeye drawing for the 21 Club, NYC.

55

NO LIE!

DR. WILLIAM MARSTON, THE PSYCHOLOGIST WHO DREAMED UP *WONDER WOMAN,* ALSO INVENTED THE *LIE DETECTOR!*

Marston.

CAUGHT BY THE AMAZON'S MAGIC LASSO--

I COMMAND YOU TO SPEAK THE TRUTH!

I AM COMPELLED TO-- I FRAMED BOTH JEFF AND TOM STONE --SO THAT THEY WOULD BE BLAMED-- FOR THE MONEY I STOLE!

ROCK...

FROCKLESS ROCK HUDSON LOVED TO READ THE FUNNIES IN HIS *BOXERS!*

Photo: Sid Avery/MPTV.

...AND ROCKER!

PHOTO-JOURNALIST *ALFRED WERTHEIMER* TRAVELED WITH *ELVIS* AND CAUGHT HIM "COVERING THE *ARCHIES!*"

Photo: Alfred Wertheiner.

TO SLEEP, PERCHANCE TO DRAW!

DURING WWI, COMMUNIST *ART YOUNG* WAS TRIED FOR *CONSPIRACY* FOR HIS ANTI-WAR CARTOONS. ALTHOUGH FACING *20 YEARS IN PRISON, YOUNG* FELL ASLEEP AT HIS TRIAL. AWAKENED BY HIS WORRIED LAWYER, *YOUNG* FLIPPANTLY DREW HIMSELF SLEEPING!

"Having Their Fling," a principle exhibit in the trial.

for Young on trial for his life

Zzzz

Commie-tose.

TO HAVE AND TO HELD!

CARTOONIST *JOHN HELD, JR.,* OFTEN CREDITED WITH INVENTING THE *FLAPPER,* WAS FREQUENTLY A *BEAUTY PAGEANT* JUDGE AND MARRIED *MISS NEW ORLEANS!*

57

Held (1889-1958) by Chuck Thorndike.

Drawn for *Weird but True* by Jan Svochak/ J. J. Sedelmaier Productions.

SLAP-HAPPY!

THE *HAWAIIAN PUNCH* AD CAMPAIGN, FEATURING *PUNCHIE* HAULING OFF AND HITTING *OAF,* WAS *TV'S* LONGEST-RUNNING GAG!

WITH FRIENDS LIKE THAT...

CLARE BRIGGS (1875-1930), THE ONLY CARTOONIST TO HAVE A *TOBACCO* NAMED AFTER HIM, DIED OF *PNEUMONIA* AFTER SUFFERING *LUNG PROBLEMS!* THE TOBACCO'S SLOGAN? *"WHEN A FELLER NEEDS A FRIEND"!*

Do you have Clare Briggs in a can?

DUMBO OR DUMBER

AFTER HIS UNSUCCESSFUL RUN FOR *PRESIDENT*, GARY HART CALLED *DISNEY'S DUMBO* *"MY CAMPAIGN DOCUMENTARY"!*

MOVE OVER, LOLITA!

PUBLICISTS FROM *FLEISCHER STUDIOS* INSISTED *BETTY BOOP* WAS ONLY *16* YEARS OLD! *WEIRD JAIL BAIT* TRUE!

58

An older but wiser Young.

QUIRKY QUOTES dept.

BLANDY AND DULLWOOD!

AFTER YEARS OF DRAWING *BLONDIE*, CHIC YOUNG (1901-1973) SUMMED UP THE CARTOONIST'S *LOT: "DRAWING A COMIC STRIP IS VERY INTERESTING IN A DULL, MONOTONOUS SORT OF WAY!"*

LIPS THAT FIT THE BILL!

POUTY BEAUTY *MICHELLE PFEIFFER* CAN'T BELIEVE WOMEN SPEND *THOUSANDS OF DOLLARS* TO HAVE THEIR LIPS *"DONE"* TO LOOK LIKE HERS! *"I LOOK LIKE DONALD DUCK,"* QUACKED *PFEIFFER* TO THE *NATIONAL ENQUIRER!*

POGO SCHTICK!

I GO POGO 1956 WALT KELLY

WHEN *POGO* RAN FOR PRESIDENT IN HIS COMIC STRIP, *MANY* READERS PLANNED ON VOTING FOR THE POSSUM! *WALT KELLY* WENT ON THE RADIO URGING LISTENERS *NOT* TO THROW AWAY THEIR VOTE— *POGO'S* CAMPAIGN WAS JUST A *JOKE!*

Walt Kelly

59

THEY'RE A PRETTY HARD ACT TO **BOOK**, CHIEF, THEY'RE IN GREAT DEMAND!

WOW

NATIONAL CARTOONISTS SOCIETY'S REUBEN for 1977

a mighty Thanks to my collegues of NCS CHESTER GOULD 7-17-78

Gould also won the National Cartoonist Society's Reuben Award...twice!

THE GOULD STANDARD

Gould.

DICK TRACY'S CHESTER GOULD WAS AWARDED A PLAQUE FROM *THE AMERICAN INSTITUTE OF MEN'S AND BOYS' WEAR* IN 1957, FOR HIS *"GOOD GROOMING* AND HIS EFFORTS TO DIVEST *YOUNG AMERICA* OF ITS *THUGGISH, SILVER-RIVETED LEATHER JACKETS"!*

THE $800 HICCUP!

MEL BLANC SPENT *16 LONG DAYS* RECORDING THE DIALOGUE FOR *GIDEON* IN *DISNEY'S PINOCCHIO.* ONLY *ONE* BARELY AUDIBLE *HICCUP* WAS USED! FOR THAT *SINGLE HICCUP, BLANC WAS PAID $800! WEIRD BURP TRUE!*

WORLD WAR TOON R dept.

THE PLANE TRUTH!

BERT CHRISTMAN, WHO DREW THE PERILOUS AVIATION ADVENTURE STRIP *SCORCHY SMITH,* WAS FATALLY GUNNED DOWN DURING HIS THIRD COMBAT MISSION IN *WORLD WAR II! WEIRD BERT TRUE!*

A prophetic panel?

SCORCHY SMITH TO FIELD--- HANG OUT THE LANTERNS -- WE'RE ALL COMIN' HOME!

ARE YOU SURE VAL ----?

TO THE MOON, CASPER!

CASPER THE FRIENDLY GHOST REALLY TOOK FLIGHT WHEN HE WAS PAINTED ON THE SIDE OF THE *APOLLO 16! WEIRD BUT BOO!*

STAY TOONED!

DURING THE *BIG* NEW YORK CITY NEWSPAPER STRIKE IN 1945, *MAYOR FIORELLO LAGUARDIA* KEPT HIS CONSTITUENTS TUNED IN BY READING THE *FUNNIES* OVER THE *RADIO!*

We have a problem, Hous-toon!

STAR POWER

NICHOLAS COPPOLA (A.K.A. CAGE) ON HOW HE CHOSE HIS STAGE NAME: "I'D ALWAYS LOVED THE COMIC BOOK CHARACTER, THE AFRICAN-AMERICAN *LUKE CAGE, POWER MAN!*"

NAME THAT TOON dept.

HOLY WATTERSON!

BILL WATTERSON'S INSPIRATION FOR NAMING *CALVIN AND HOBBES* WAS RELIGIOUS REFORMER *JOHN CALVIN* AND PHILOSOPHER *THOMAS HOBBES!*

A self-caricature by Watterson.

61

MERRIE MONIKERS!

THE NAME OF THE TEAM WHO PRODUCED THE EARLY MUSICAL MADCAPS *LOONEY TUNES* AND *MERRIE MELODIES?* *HUGH HARMON* AND *RUDY ISING.* *HARMON-ISING!* GET IT?!

GRIM REALITY!

BETTY BOOP CREATOR GRIM NATWICK, WHO PASSED THE ENTRANCE EXAM TO THE SAME ART ACADEMY THAT REJECTED ADOLF HITLER, OFTEN WONDERED IF WORLD HISTORY WOULD HAVE BEEN DIFFERENT IF HITLER HAD BEEN ACCEPTED INSTEAD OF HIM!

Adolph and his rejected art.

Grim and his respected tart.

Villains don't have a prayer against Japan's turbo-charged toon, Astroboy!

TEMPLE OF TOON!

A TOON TEMPLE EXISTS OUTSIDE TOKYO WHERE BUDDHISTS OFFER PRAYERS TO TOONS AND CARTOONISTS!

IT'S A BIRD! IT'S A PLANE! UH...IT'S A BIRD!

MOVIE COSTUME DESIGNER ALBA BALLARD OF LONG ISLAND HAS MADE OVER 400 TINY OUTFITS FOR HER PET BIRDS! THIS SUPERMAN IS ACTUALLY A TRUSSED UP "COCKATOON"!

THE BUTT OF A JOKE

PARISIAN CARTOONIST *JEAN VEBER'S* (1864-1928) WORK PROVOKED AN OFFICIAL OUTCRY, BUT HE REFUSED TO CAVE IN. *VEBER FEARLESSLY* WENT ON TO CREATE HIS MOST FAMOUS PIECE, *L'IMPUDIQUE ALBION* (SHAMELESS ALBION), FEATURING *KING EDWARD VII'S* FACE ON THE *REAR END* OF *BRITANNIA!*

WEIRD BUTT TRUE!

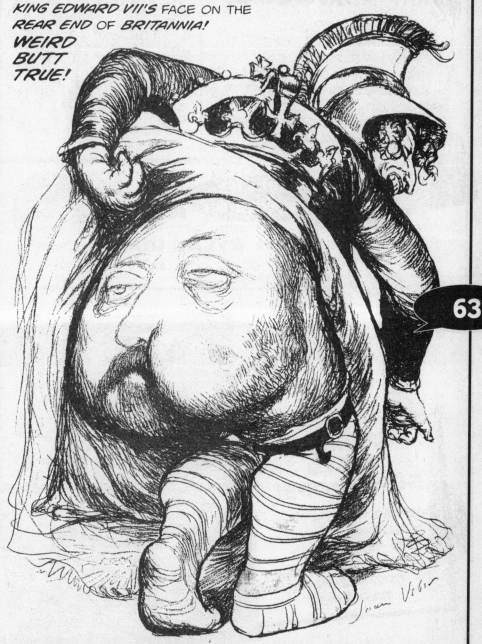

Ward.

For Craig

Art by John Stanley.

VERY aMOOSing!

JAY WARD GOT *BULLWINKLE'S* NAME FROM A BERKELEY, CAL., USED CAR SALESMAN NAMED *CLARENCE BULLWINKLE!* *WARD'S* CO-WORKER RECALLED, *"JAY* THOUGHT *BULLWINKLE'S* NAME WAS *HILARIOUS!"*

★ celebrity cartoonist ★ dept.

A cur-toon?

DYLAN DOG!
DOGGY DOO-DLE BY *BOB DYLAN!*

64

SUPERHERO MEETS SUPERMODEL

FLESH MET FANTASY WHEN *CLAUDIA SCHIFFER* GOT TANGLED UP IN *SPIDER-MAN'S* WEB IN *MOUTH-2-MOUTH MAGAZINE!*

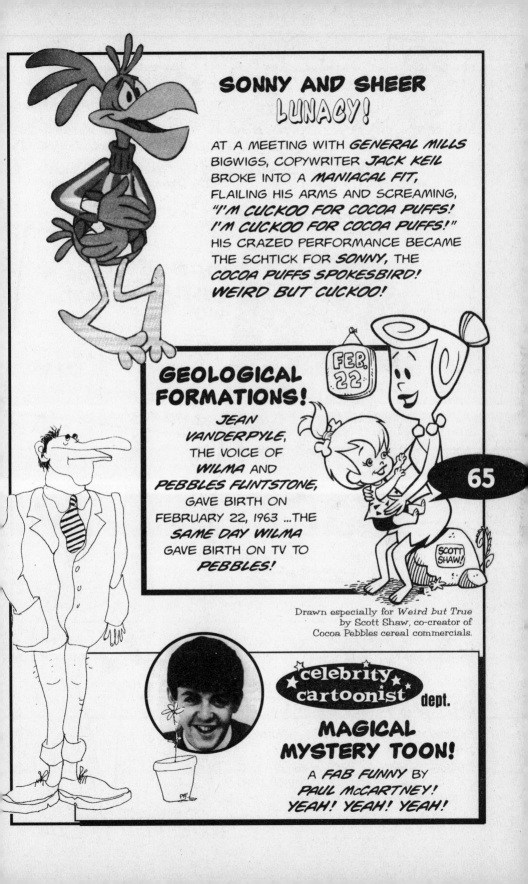

SONNY AND SHEER LUNACY!

AT A MEETING WITH *GENERAL MILLS* BIGWIGS, COPYWRITER *JACK KEIL* BROKE INTO A *MANIACAL FIT*, FLAILING HIS ARMS AND SCREAMING, *"I'M CUCKOO FOR COCOA PUFFS! I'M CUCKOO FOR COCOA PUFFS!"* HIS CRAZED PERFORMANCE BECAME THE SCHTICK FOR *SONNY*, THE *COCOA PUFFS SPOKESBIRD! WEIRD BUT CUCKOO!*

GEOLOGICAL FORMATIONS!

JEAN VANDERPYLE, THE VOICE OF *WILMA* AND *PEBBLES FLINTSTONE*, GAVE BIRTH ON FEBRUARY 22, 1963 ...THE *SAME DAY WILMA* GAVE BIRTH ON TV TO *PEBBLES!*

FEB. 22

SCOTT SHAW!

65

Drawn especially for *Weird but True* by Scott Shaw, co-creator of Cocoa Pebbles cereal commercials.

★ celebrity cartoonist ★ dept.

MAGICAL MYSTERY TOON!

A *FAB FUNNY* BY *PAUL McCARTNEY!* YEAH! YEAH! YEAH!

MODERN TOONS!

CHARLIE CHAPLIN SHOE CANE DRAW!

Charlie Chaplin

66

KISS GIVES SELFLESSLY FOR A WORTHY CAUSE!

REAL BLOOD EXTRACTED FROM THE MEMBERS OF THE ROCK BAND *KISS* WAS MIXED INTO THE INK USED TO PRINT THE *KISS MARVEL COMIC BOOK!*

OL' WET NOSE!

SCOOBY-DOO'S NAME CAME FROM THE POPULAR *SINATRA* SONG *"STRANGERS IN THE NIGHT."* THE CHORUS WAS *"DOOBY DOOBY DOO"*! *WEIRD BUT DOG-DOO!*

Lee Phalk...er, Falk.

LEE FALK

LUKE

PHACT!

ACCORDING TO *PHANTOM* CREATOR *LEE FALK*, DURING THE GERMAN OCCUPATION OF NORWAY, *NAZIS* WERE REPORTING IN *NAZI-CONTROLLED* NEWSPAPERS THAT THE *U.S.* HAD *FALLEN*. BUT *NORWEGIANS* KNEW THAT WAS A LIE BECAUSE THE AMERICAN STRIP *THE PHANTOM* WAS STILL APPEARING REGULARLY IN THOSE *SAME* DAILY PAPERS!

Drawn for *Weird but True* by *Phantom* comic book artist Luke McDonnell.

AU REVOIR, TINTIN!

FRANCE MOURNED THE DEATH OF *HERGÉ*, THE BELOVED *TINTIN* CREATOR. TO HONOR HIM, THE NEWSPAPER *LIBÉRATION* USED *HERGÉ'S* ART TO ILLUSTRATE *EVERY* STORY, FROM *POLITICAL EVENTS* TO *TV* AND *WEATHER*!

Hergé (1907-1983).

Libération

LA DERNIÈRE AVENTURE DE TINTIN

FRANCE, RFA VOTES EN STOCK

WAAOOOUUUUUH TINTIN EST MORT

"JANE, STOP THIS CRAZY THING!"

IN SOME *JETSONS* EPISODES, *GEORGE* AND *JANE* HAD *SEPARATE* BEDS, IN OTHERS THE BEDS WERE *PUSHED TOGETHER,* AND IN STILL OTHERS THEY *SLEPT IN THE SAME BED! TALK ABOUT BEDLAM!*

BRAVISSIMO!

THIS DRAWING BY *FEDERICO FELLINI* IS OF HIS WIFE, THE STAR OF *LA STRADA, GIULIETTA MASINA!*

68

THE KISS-OFF?

HENRY KISSINGER ON *GARRY TRUDEAU'S DOONESBURY:* "THE ONLY THING WORSE THAN BEING IN IT WOULD BE *NOT TO BE IN IT!*"

WEIRD BUT TRUDEAU!

WORDS TO LIVE BY!

NANCY CARTOONIST *ERNIE BUSHMILLER* ADVISED HIS ASSISTANTS TO *"DUMB IT DOWN!"*

WELL-- WHO'S GOT A GAG FOR ME TODAY?

ERNIE BUSHMILLER

Drawing the line in Mississippi

B?

TEDDY COULDN'T BEAR IT!

TEDDY ROOSEVELT'S REFUSAL TO SHOOT A BEAR CUB IN 1902 INSPIRED A CARTOONIST TO INVENT THE TEDDY BEAR! *THE CARTOONIST'S NAME?* CLIFFORD BERRYMAN! WEIRD BEAR TRUE!

A Berryman self-portrait, circa 1923.

celebrity cartoonist dept.

FROM THE BACHELOR (DRAWING) PAD!

A CARTOON BY THE WORLD'S MOST FAMOUS PLAYBOY, *HUGH HEFNER!*

THE ART INSTITUTE

STUDENTS O

Hef

"Man—is she stacked!"

ISSUED IN CONJUNCTION WITH THE "FELIX THE CAT" CARTOONS APPEARING EXCLUSIVELY IN PATHÉS "EVE & EVERYBODY'S FILM REVIEW"

FELIX KEPT ON WALKING

WORDS BY E? E BRYANT

MUSIC BY HUBERT W. DAVID

Copyright.

Price 6? net

PUSSY POWER!

IN GREAT BRITAIN IN 1923 *"FELIX KEPT ON WALKING,"* BY *BRYANT* AND *DAVID,* WAS THE #1 SONG!

WORLD WAR W TOON R dept.

"Joe, yestiddy ya saved my life an' I swore I'd pay ya back. Here's my last pair of dry socks."

FROM THE HEART!

HIT BY A *SHELL FRAGMENT* AT SALERNO, ITALY, SOLDIER CARTOONIST *BILL* (*WILLIE* AND *JOE*) *MAULDIN* WAS AWARDED THE *PURPLE HEART!*

An unpublished self-caricature by Mauldin, circa 1947.

SEDUCTION OF THE INNOCENT dept.

A COUPLE MORE MILES OUGHTA DO TH' TRICK!

IT BETTER! THESE GRAVEL ROADS ARE TOUGH ON TIRES!

BUT YA GOTTA ADMIT, THERE'S NOTHING LIKE 'EM FOR ERASING FACES!

SUPERB! EVEN BIG PHIL WILL ADMIRE THIS JOB—IF HE LIVES LONG ENOUGH TO IDENTIFY THE MEAT!

THEN *LITTLE MIKE* TURK WOULD COME ROARING BACK!

Wertham.

A TOON WITHOUT PITY!

DR. FREDRIC WERTHAM DIAGNOSED THE STATE OF COMICS THUS: "DRAGGING *LIVING* PEOPLE TO *DEATH* IS DESCRIBED *WITHOUT PITY* IN CHILDREN'S COMICS"!

HE ALSO HAD A HAND IN CARTOONING!

A RARE, UNPUBLISHED CARTOON BY *MUPPET* MASTER *JIM HENSON!*

The author with Jim Henson and friends.

HAPPY ACCIDENT TO HAPPY TRAILS!

DING'S CARTOON COMMEMORATING THE DEATH OF *TEDDY ROOSEVELT* WAS ALMOST *NEVER PUBLISHED!* *DING* DREW IT, THEN THREW IT AWAY. BUT IT WAS RETRIEVED TO MEET THE DEADLINE. THIS ALMOST *REJECTED* CARTOON BECAME *DING'S MOST POPULAR EVER!*

71

"The Long, Long Trail."

★celebrity★ ★cartoonist★ dept.

DIDN'T HE ALSO DRAW PAT the BOONY?

PAT BOONE DREW A FEATURE CALLED *A BOONE CARTOON* FOR HIS OWN *DC COMIC BOOK!*

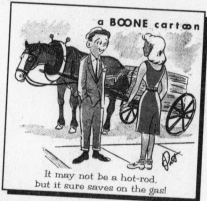

It may not be a hot-rod, but it sure saves on the gas!

"Touché!"

Self-caricature by Thurber.

BLIND AMBITION!

CARTOONIST *JAMES THURBER* WAS *LEGALLY BLIND!*

WORLD WAR TOONR dept.

MY SON, THE SUPERHERO!

THE *NAZI* PROPAGANDA TOOL *DAS SCHWARTZ* BRANDED *SUPERMAN* A *JEW!*

THE ROAST IS HISTORY!

IN 1916, *PLANTERS PEANUTS* HELD A CONTEST TO CREATE A COMPANY SPOKESTOON WITH A *$5 PRIZE-MERE PEANUTS!* THE WINNING ENTRY WAS *13-YEAR-OLD ANTONIO GENTILE'S MR. PEANUT! NUTTY BUT TRUE!*

HOW TO DRAW SEVEN CIRCLES
BY SEYMOUSE CHWAST

STEP 1. STEP 2.

STEP 3. STEP 4.

Art by Seymour Chwast for
The Art of Mickey Mouse.

BOSOM BUDDY!

DISNEY ARTIST *JOHN HENCH* ON THE POPULARITY OF *MICKEY:*

"...MICKEY MOUSE...IS MADE OUT OF A SERIES OF CIRCLES...CIRCLES ARE THINGS WE HAVE FUN WITH – BABIES, WOMEN'S BEHINDS, BREASTS!"

73

Barney Google in "Horse Flesh."
You don't want to know!

V. FUZZYNUTS Presents —
BARNEY GOOGLE IN HORSE FLESH
Elmer Fritch

EYE POPPING!

IN THE *1930'S* AND *1940'S, UNAUTHORIZED PORNOGRAPHIC* MINI-COMICS CALLED *TIJUANA BIBLES* ("THE KIND *MEN* LIKE!") FEATURED SOME OF THE *BIGGEST CARTOON STARS OF THE DAY, AMONG THEM, JIGGS, BETTY BOOP, POPEYE,* AND *BATMAN!*

A very Avery by Avery!

An animator by Blair.

DON'T TAKE IT OFF!

DIRECTOR *TEX AVERY* AND ANIMATOR *PRESTON BLAIR* TURNED OUT SOME OF THE *SEXIEST* CARTOONS OF *ALL TIME!* A 1943 THEATER AUDIENCE IN ISELIN, N.J., CLAPPED, WHISTLED, AND *YELLED* UNTIL THE BELEAGUERED MANAGER SHOWED ONE OF THEIR *HOT* TOONS *THREE TIMES!*

Dunn (far right) and fellow cartoonists in drag at a National Cartoonists Society meeting. Weird but tutu.

Knock-Knock first, 1936.

NYUK NYUK!

KNOCK KNOCK! WHO'S THERE? *BOB DUNN!* BOB DUNN *WHO?* CARTOONIST BOB DUNN GONE AND INVENTED THE *KNOCK-KNOCK JOKE!*

Dunn created this Knock-Knock joke especially for *Weird but True*.

TWIN TOONS dept.

TOON AFTER TOON!

MAYBE *CYNDI* AND *CRUELLA* ARE THE SAME PERSON...HAVE YOU EVER SEEN THEM *TOGETHER?!*

Cyndi Lauper.   Cruella De Vil.

BELLY LAFFS!

A *PRUDISH* SYNDICATE EDITOR USED TO CENSOR ALL THE *BELLY BUTTONS* IN *BEETLE BAILEY!* *MORT WALKER* FOUGHT BACK BY GIVING *MULTIPLE* BELLY BUTTONS TO THE TOONS UNTIL THE *EXASPERATED BLUENOSE* EDITOR GAVE UP HIS *NAVEL MANEUVERS! WEIRD BELLY BUTTON TRUE!*

75

Miss Buxley's navel can now be innie the newspapers. Drawn for *Weird but True* by Mort Walker.

WHAT'S DA BIG IDEA MAKIN' US LOOK LIKE SUCH *IDIOTS?*

YEAH! YOU GOT US ACTIN' LIKE WE'RE A BUNCH OF *KNUCKLE-HEADS!*

RIGHT! WE'RE *MORONS* AND WE DON'T WANNA BE DRAWN AS ANYTHING *BUT MORONS!*

THE FOURTH STOOGE!

CARTOONIST *NORMAN MAURER* DREW 3-D *THREE STOOGES* COMIC BOOKS, WROTE, PRODUCED AND DIRECTED *THREE STOOGES* MOVIES, AND *MARRIED MOE'S DAUGHTER! NYUK! NYUK!*

WORLD WAR TOON dept.

Russell Patterson as he saw himself.

WAC-KY!

CARTOONIST **RUSSELL PATTERSON** DESIGNED THE UNIFORMS FOR THE **WACS!**

NAME THAT TOON dept.

76

HIS NAME IS MUD!

ELMER FUDD'S NAME CAME FROM THE 1920'S HIT SONG, *"MISSISSIPPI MUD"*: "IT'S A TREAT TO MEET YOU ON THE MISSISSIPPI MUD... *UNCLE FUDD"!*

BETTER LUCK NEXT TIME!

AFTER CREATING THE *BIGGEST* COMIC BOOK PANEL *EVER* AT *3' BY 5'6"*, *BARRY WINDSOR-SMITH* SAID HE HOPED IT WOULD GET HIM INTO *WEIRD BUT TRUE TOON FACTOIDS!*

NO KIDDING?!

WILLIAM RANDOLPH HEARST III SAID OF HIS GRANDFATHER'S SENSATIONALIST NEWSPAPER ERA, "...IT WAS THE YELLOW KID WHO SUPPLIED THE IMAGE FOR THE PHRASE 'YELLOW JOURNALISM'; NOT AN EDITOR, REPORTER, OR PROPRIETOR, BUT A CARTOON NAMED THIS PHENOMENON!"

The Kid ...

... and Hearst.

An unpublished drawing. Hmm...Did the Yellow Kid grow up to be Uncle Fester?

A self-portrait, circa 1937.

FAMILY RESEMBLANCE!

CARTOONIST CHARLES ADDAMS, WHO ORIGINATED THE ADDAMS FAMILY IN HIS NEW YORKER CARTOONS, REVEALED, "UNCLE FESTER...IS, IN EFFECT, ME, BECAUSE I THINK HE LOOKS LIKE ME, OR THAT'S THE WAY I FEEL THAT I LOOK, PLUS A LITTLE MORE HAIR!"

YOU'RE NEVER TOO OLD TO STRIP!

CARL ANDERSON (1865-1948) WAS ABOUT TO CELEBRATE HIS 70TH BIRTHDAY WHEN HIS HENRY COMIC STRIP BEGAN!

Was Carl Anderson the Grandma Moses of comics?

An unpublished drawing by Henry's creator.

SLANGUAGE!*

WE HAVE *SILK HAT HARRY* CREATOR *TAD* TO THANK FOR MUCH OF THE POPULAR SLANG OF THE *1920'S* AND *1930'S* INCLUDING:

- *BALL AND CHAIN* (WIFE)
- *BUTTINSKY* (MEDDLER)
- *CAT'S MEOW* (WONDERFUL)
- *DOGS* (FEET)
- *APPLESAUCE* (NONSENSE)
- *CHEW THE FAT* (TALK OVER)
- *WINDBAG* (BRAGGART)

A rare drawing of T. A. Dorgan by *Krazy Kat's* creator, George Herriman.

WORLD WAR TOON dept.

JOE PALOOKA
COPYRIGHT DEFEATER
IN THE ARMY
10¢

HAF A HEART, JOE —MINE GOOSE STEP AIN'T VOT IT USED TO BE!

G.I. JOE!

THE *BRITISH MINISTRY OF INFORMATION* KEPT *HAM "JOE PALOOKA" FISHER* INFORMED OF *GENERAL MONTGOMERY'S* PROGRESS IN THE *BATTLE OF TUNISIA* SO THE ACTUAL BATTLE AND THE CARTOON VERSION MIGHT *END* AT THE *SAME TIME!*

Ham and Joe.

INSTEAD OF A SELF PORTRAIT I HAD PALOOKA DRAW ME!

* Cartoonist Will Gould coined the word *slanguage* in 1926 in a feature drawn about Tad!

THINKING **BIG!**

BIG BOY WAS INSPIRED BY 6-YEAR-OLD **RICHARD WOODRUFF,** WHO WORE DROOPY OVERALLS AND SWEPT UP IN THE **ORIGINAL** RESTAURANT IN EXCHANGE FOR HAMBURGERS. THE ARTIST WHO SKETCHED THE FIRST CONCEPTS OF **BIG BOY** WAS **BEN WASHAM,** A **LOONEY TUNES** ANIMATOR!

Big Ben.

Unca Donald by the "Good Duck Artist," Carl Barks.

79

FOWL PLAY!

THE DONALD WAS BROUGHT UP ON **MORALS CHARGES** IN **FINLAND** FOR HIS 50-YEAR ENGAGEMENT TO **DAISY** AND QUESTIONABLE PARENTAGE OF HIS **NEPHEWS HUEY, DEWEY,** AND **LOUIE!**

A self-caricature by Vip.

FIGURES IN THE DOUBLE DIGITS!

CARTOONIST **VIP** DREW **7-FINGERED** HANDS IN HIS **SURREAL** TOONS! HE EXPLAINED HE WAS MAKING UP FOR ALL THE YEARS HE WAS **FORCED** TO DRAW **4-FINGERED** MICE AND DUCKS WHILE HE WORKED FOR **DISNEY!**

PRAISE THE LORD AND PASS THE PEANUTS!

THEOLOGIAN *ROBERT SHORT* FINANCED HIS EDUCATION BY GIVING LECTURES ON THE *THEOLOGICAL IMPLICATIONS* OF *PEANUTS!*

A rare Schulz drawing.

I'D GIVE ANYTHING IN THE WORLD IF I COULD GO TO SUNDAY SCHOOL!

SCHULZ

'BYE NOW...IT'S BEEN WONDERFUL KNOWING YOU.

Ding did Ding doing Ding.

DING DONE!

DING DREW THIS CARTOON IN *1958* TO COMMEMORATE *HIS OWN DEATH!* DING'S SECRETARY *HID* IT UNTIL HIS *DEMISE* IN *1962!*

THE JIGGS WAS UP (FOR VOTE)!

WHEN *GEORGE McMANUS'S JIGGS* AND *MAGGIE* TOOK A TRIP AROUND THE WORLD IN 1937, FOREIGN OFFICIALS REQUESTED THE COUPLE VISIT THEIR COUNTRIES AS *GOODWILL AMBASSADORS!* THE MOTION WAS SECONDED IN *CONGRESS!*

McManus by
Henry Major.

81

Frank Willard by
Billy DeBeck, 1935.

TOO OLD TO BE A JUVENILE DELINQUENT!

A *CANADIAN PREMIER* COMPLAINED THAT *FRANK WILLARD'S MOON MULLINS*, WHICH BEGAN IN 1923, SET A BAD EXAMPLE FOR CANADA'S YOUTH, BUT ADMITTED TO READING THE STRIP HIMSELF, ONLY BECAUSE HE WAS *PAST THE AGE IT COULD DO HIM HARM!*

MOON MULLINS
by Frank Willard

LOOKOUT!

CRAYON AND PAINT BOOK

COPYRIGHT 1938
McLOUGHLIN BROS. INC.
SPRINGFIELD, MASS.
MADE IN U.S.A.
2051

dept.

Clampett by
Tex Avery.

IT'S THE OTHER WHITE MEAT!

BOB CLAMPETT (1913-1984) WAS ASKED FOR IDEAS FOR AN ANIMAL VERSION OF *OUR GANG*, WHICH HAD A CHUBBY LITTLE BOY (*SPANKY*) AND A CUTE KID NAMED AFTER FOOD (*BUCKWHEAT*). *CLAMPETT*, IMITATING THE LETTERING OF A CAN OF *CAMPBELL'S*, SKETCHED A FAT LITTLE PIG NAMED *PORKY* AND A CAT NAMED *BEANS*. HE THEN WROTE *"CLAMPETT'S PORKY AND BEANS!"*

BOB CLAMPETT

82

THEY'RE KEENE FOR KATY!

MANY FAMOUS FASHION DESIGNERS, INCLUDING *ANNA SUI*, CITE *BILL WOGGON'S* COMIC BOOK CUTIE *KATY KEENE* AS AN EARLY INFLUENCE. ALL OF *KATY'S* OUTFITS WERE DESIGNED BY HER YOUNG ADORING *FANS!*

Self-caricature drawn for
Weird but True.

Note how kid designers are
given credit at the bottom
of this comic page.

KATY KEENE by BILL WOGGON

KATY'S ROCKET PIN-UP FASHION-POSE DESIGNED BY THESE FANS...
BARBARA BAUSCH,   FRANCES SPERL,   ALETA FAYE DAVIDSON,
1878 OXTALPA   403 LACLEDE AVE.   507 FERRY ST.,
BERKLEY MICH.   COLORADO SPRINGS, COLO.   METROPOLIS, ILL.
and MARILYN KAYE MITTENDORF, 1610 NORTH AVE., METROPOLIS, ILL.
LETTERING AT TOP DESIGNED by KITTIE JAMES, 68 WELDON ST, BROOKLYN 8, NEW YORK. (AGE 17)

QUIRKY QUOTES dept.

SPIT-TOON!

WHEN *REN AND STIMPY* CREATOR *JOHN KRICFALUSI* PITCHED HIS IDEA TO THE NETWORKS, "...THEY JUST WANTED TO *CALL THE GUARDS*...I WAS JUMPING AROUND, *HOOTING* AND *SCREAMING* AND *SPITTING* ON THEM AND STUFF, ACTING THE WHOLE THING OUT. IT WAS LIKE, *'HOW CAN WE GET THIS GUY OUT OF THE ROOM?!'*"

"WHO STOLE THE PEOPLE'S MONEY?" — DO TELL. N.Y.TIMES.   'TWAS HIM.

TIME TO GET NASTY!

THIS *THOMAS NAST* (1840-1902) CARTOON SO ANGERED ITS TARGET, *WILLIAM "BOSS" TWEED* (FRONT LEFT), THAT ONE OF HIS THUGS "SUGGESTED" THAT *NAST* ACCEPT *$100,000* TO "STUDY ART" IN EUROPE. *NAST* GOT HIM UP TO A *HALF MILLION DOLLARS*, AND THEN RETORTED, "I DON'T THINK I'LL GO TO EUROPE. I MADE UP MY MIND TO PUT SOME OF THOSE FELLOWS *BEHIND BARS*, AND I'M *GOING* TO PUT THEM THERE!" *AND SO HE DID!*

BAD HARE DAY!

FAME HAS GONE TO *ROGER RABBIT'S* HEAD! *DISNEY'S HEAD HONCHO, MICHAEL EISNER,* COMPLAINS, "WE ARE ALL GETTING TIRED OF SENDING HIM FLOWERS... COMPLIMENTING HIS ACTING, AND *RENEGOTIATING HIS DEAL!*"

OUT OF THE INKWELL AND INTO THE PEN!

AFTER BEING EXPOSED IN *THOMAS NAST'S* SCATHING CARTOONS, CORRUPT POLITICAL "BOSS" *WILLIAM TWEED* FLED TO SPAIN TO AVOID *PRISON.* BUT, *TWEED* WAS NABBED BY *SPANISH POLICE* WHO HAD RECOGNIZED HIM FROM THIS *NAST CARTOON!*

84

Drawn especially for *Weird but True* by Dondi and Annie artists, Irwin Hasen and Tex Blaisdell.

EYE-YI-YI! PART I

ACCORDING TO *MAD MAGAZINE,* BETWEEN THEM, *DONDI* AND *LITTLE ORPHAN ANNIE* COULD EACH HAVE *ONE GOOD EYE!*

SMELLS LIKE TOON SPIRIT!

PULITZER PRIZE WINNING CARTOONIST *JULES FEIFFER'S* FIRST JOB WAS ASSISTING *WILL EISNER*, CREATOR OF THE *SPIRIT.* ONE OF *FEIFFER'S* DUTIES INCLUDED SIGNING EISNER'S NAME TO THE ART! WHEN *FEIFFER* ENTERED THE ARMY, *EISNER* SIGNED THE WORK HIMSELF. NEWSPAPER EDITORS *SMELLED SOMETHING WRONG* AND INQUIRED IF *EISNER HAD DIED!*

Drawn—and signed—by Will Eisner especially for *Weird but True!*

OR MAYBE IT WAS A BOO BOO?

85

BASEBALL'S *YOGI BERRA* THREATENED TO SUE OVER *YOGI BEAR'S* NAME! *HANNA-BARBERA SWORE* THE SIMILARITY WAS *PURELY COINCIDENTAL!*

Art by Plastic Man's Jack Cole.

Wertham, by Henry Major.

SEDUCTION OF THE INNOCENT dept.

EYE-YI-YI! PART 2

1950'S *ANTI-COMIC BOOK* CRUSADER *DR. FREDERIC WERTHAM* CALLED THIS PANEL *"A SAMPLE OF THE INJURY-TO-THE-EYE MOTIF!"*

HIGH ON LOIS!

SUPERMAN WRITER *JERRY SIEGEL* ADMITTED THE INSPIRATION FOR *LOIS LANE* CAME FROM A HIGH SCHOOL GIRL HE HAD A CRUSH ON... *LOIS AMSTER!* HERE IS *SUPERMAN* ARTIST *JOE SHUSTER'S* PORTRAIT OF A SMOLDERING *LOIS!* *HUBBA HUBBA!*

DEAD LETTER OFFICE!

IT'S TRUE! THE GUMPS' *SIDNEY SMITH* WAS FLOODED WITH MAIL WHEN HE PENNED THE DEATH OF *MARY GOLD* IN 1929, CREATING THE FIRST *TOON DEATH!*

MICHAEL
MOUSE!

*THE KING OF POP ART?
MICKEY MOUSE BY
MICHAEL JACKSON.*

From the
author's book,
*The Art of
Mickey Mouse.*

"How can you marry
a man with lots of
money? As soon as
you marry him it
will be gone!"

FROM BAWDY TO BARBIE!

GERMAN MEN LOVED *LILLI*, THE *"SYMBOL OF
ILLICIT SEX"*! THIS *TAWDRY TOON* DEBUTED
IN *BILD ZEITUNG* IN 1952. SHE WAS THEN
FASHIONED INTO A *DOLL* AND
BOUGHT BY MEN IN *TOBACCO
SHOPS! RUTH HANDLER*
BROUGHT A *LILLI* DOLL FROM
EUROPE AND *COPIED* HER TO
MAKE A DOLL FOR *LITTLE
GIRLS.* SHE NAMED HER
BARBIE...THE REST IS
HER-STORY!

87

From the author's book,
The Art of Barbie.

CAR-TOON!

AN OBSESSED *SMOKEY STOVER* FAN,
PETE SCHLATTER, BUILT A *REAL-LIFE*
TWO-WHEELED *FOOMOBILE!*
WEIRD BUT FOO!

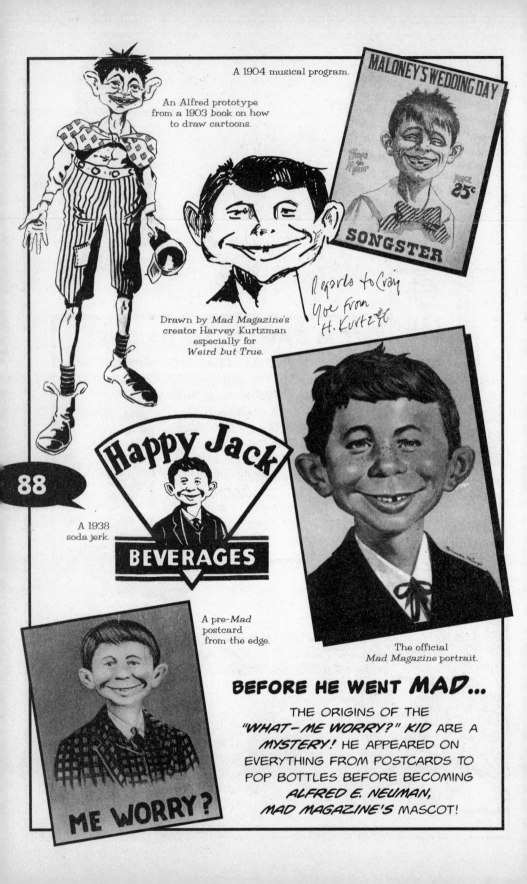

An Alfred prototype from a 1903 book on how to draw cartoons.

A 1904 musical program.

MALONEY'S WEDDING DAY

PRICE 25¢

SONGSTER

Drawn by *Mad Magazine's* creator Harvey Kurtzman especially for *Weird but True.*

Regards to Craig Yoe from H. Kurtzman

88

Happy Jack
BEVERAGES

A 1938 soda jerk.

A pre-*Mad* postcard from the edge.

The official *Mad Magazine* portrait.

ME WORRY?

BEFORE HE WENT *MAD*...

THE ORIGINS OF THE *"WHAT—ME WORRY?"* KID ARE A *MYSTERY!* HE APPEARED ON EVERYTHING FROM POSTCARDS TO POP BOTTLES BEFORE BECOMING *ALFRED E. NEUMAN, MAD MAGAZINE'S* MASCOT!

"PLEASE REST AWHILE, MISTER-- YOU'VE BEEN TOWING US FOR HOURS!"

"YEAH-- *PUFF-PUFF-- --IT IS KINDA TIRING!*"

TO CRAIG-- MY BEST FRIEND-- PALS-- Boody Rogers

WORLD WAR TOON R dept.

SHAKIN' BOODY!

HAVING A *PREMONITION* HE'D *NEVER* RETURN FROM WWII, *BOODY ROGERS* ENDED HIS STRIP BY APPARENTLY DROWNING ITS STAR, *SPARKY WATTS!* BUT, *BOODY* DID RETURN AND *SPARKY* WAS REBORN TO EMBARK ON *NEW ADVENTURES!*

He's in the army now, at Camp Hood, teaching about camouflage.

celebrity cartoonist dept.

MAKING HIS MARK!

LEGENDARY AMERICAN AUTHOR *MARK TWAIN!*

89

SEDUCTION OF THE INNOCENT dept.

STRIP POKER!

ABOUT THIS *SHOCKING* COMIC BOOK PANEL, *DR. FREDRIC WERTHAM, M.D.,* SAID, *"CHILDREN* TOLD ME WHAT THE MAN WAS GOING TO DO WITH THE *RED-HOT POKER"!*

Springtime.

Kley.

FEAT of KLEY!

HEINRICH KLEY, A CARTOONIST KNOWN FOR DRAWING THE
BIZARRE, WAS REPORTED *DEAD* SO MANY TIMES
IN THE 1940'S AND 1950'S, IT'S SAID THAT
NO ONE KNOWS WHEN HE *REALLY* DIED...
OR DID HE?

"YOU MEAN I'M SUPPOSED TO STAND ON THAT?"

HERBALISM!

HERB BLOCK, WHO USED
THE PEN NAME *HERBLOCK*
SINCE AGE 13, COINED THE
WORD *McCARTHYISM* IN
THE 1950'S IN THIS CARTOON!

NAME THAT TOON dept.

DID BOYER PUT UP A STINK?

PEPE LE PEW'S NAME CAME FROM *PEPE LE MOKO*, A CHARACTER PLAYED BY *CHARLES BOYER* IN THE 1938 FILM *ALGIERS!* WEIRD BUT PEW!

FOUR PLAY!

IN 1922, THE 4 *ROTH BROTHERS* CAME FROM VIENNA PLAYING WITH THE IDEA OF DRAWING *FUNNY PICTURES.* ALL 4 BECAME SUCCESSFUL MAGAZINE GAG CARTOONISTS... TOGETHER THEY PRODUCED OVER *80 IDEAS A WEEK!*

IT'S SAD, REALLY...

A *MICKEY*-BELIA-COLLECTING, *PRINCESS DI*-WORSHIPPING *NUT-JOB* FROM PEEKSKILL, N.Y., HAS OFFERED TO PAY *ONE MILLION DOLLARS* FOR THIS *MICKEY SWEATSHIRT* WORN BY THE LATE, GREAT *PRINCESS!*

MICKEY MOO

...IS *MICKEY MOUSE'S* PET *COW!* SHE WAS BORN WITH MICKEY'S SILHOUETTE ON HER SIDE! *WEIRD BUT MOO!*

HOW TWEET!
FACT!

ANIMATOR *BOB CLAMPETT* CLAIMED HIS *BABY PICTURE* WAS THE INSPIRATION FOR *TWEETY BIRD!*

EAT YOUR SUSHI OR YOU'LL HAVE TO WATCH MORE CARTOONS!

OVER *700* JAPANESE CHILDREN SUFFERED *CONVULSIVE SEIZURES* AND *NAUSEA* WATCHING THE POPULAR TV CARTOON *POKEMON,* DUE TO ITS *BRIGHT, FLASHING SCENES!* THE SHOW WAS PROMPTLY *CANCELED,* AND VIDEOS *BANNED* FROM STORES!

THE DEVIL MADE HIM DO IT!

THIS *BIZARRE* ENGRAVING BY 16TH CENTURY GERMAN ARTIST *ERHARD SCHÖN* DEPICTING *MARTIN LUTHER* AS AN INSTRUMENT OF *THE DEVIL* IS MOST LIKELY THE *FIRST* CARICATURE *EVER USED IN PRINT!*

93

SHRINK RAP!

RESPECTED PSYCHIATRIST *DR. CAROLE LEIBERMAN* TOLD THE *NATIONAL ENQUIRER* THAT *BEAVIS AND BUTTHEAD* "...IS *SESAME STREET* FOR *FUTURE SOCIOPATHS!"*

By Bryon Moore for the book *The Art of Barbie* by Craig Yoe.

DA-DOODle RON RON!

ACTOR-PRESIDENT *RONALD REAGAN'S* CARTOONING TALENT IS REVEALED IN THIS *DEFT DOODLE!*

EEK! A MOUSE!

THE DAY *MICHAEL JACKSON* WED *LISA MARIE*, HE SPORTED A *FLINTSTONES TIE* AND WORE *MICKEY MOUSE PJ'S* ON HIS *HONEYMOON!*

94

YO, CRAIG!

YOUR PAL, MATT GROENING 8·15·1992

ICE-Y RECEPTION!

YO! BART SIMPSON HAD A SMASH HIT WITH HIS RAP SONG *DO THE BARTMAN,* BUT HAD A MAJOR DETRACTOR: RAPPER *VANILLA ICE. ICE* COLDLY REMARKED, *"RAPPING AIN'T NO JOKE." BART* REPLIED THAT THE CRITIQUE HURT HIM, BUT *"VANILLA ICE* REMAINS ONE OF MY *FAVORITE FLAVORS!"*

CARTOONS STINK!

RUBE GOLDBERG REMINISCED, "I SHALL NEVER FORGET THE *EXCITEMENT* I EXPERIENCED WHEN I FIRST... INHALED THE FRAGRANT AROMA OF *PRINTER'S INK,* GALLOPING OVER... *T.S. SULLIVANT, ZIM, ALBERT LEVERING, KEPPLER, GILLAM, GIBSON,* AND OTHERS. I LITERALLY HELD THE MAGAZINES CLOSE TO MY FACE SO THAT I MIGHT *INHALE* THE TALENTS OF THOSE CARTOONISTS WHOSE WORK I ADMIRED WITH AN *ADOLESCENT ECSTASY!"* WEIRD BUT *P.U.!*

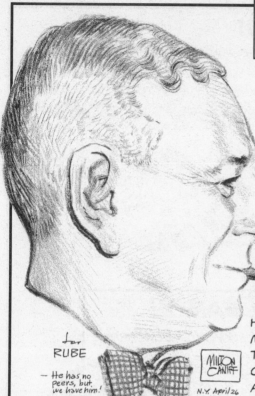

for RUBE

— He has no peers, but we have him!

MILTON CANIFF

N.Y. April 26 1966

Rube, a smell fellow, by Milton Caniff.

95

IT'S BEGINNING TO LOOK A LOT LIKE FATHER CHRISTMAS!

YES, VIRGINIA, IN *HARPER'S WEEKLY* IN 1866, *THOMAS NAST* ORIGINATED THE MODERN CONCEPT OF THE *SANTA* WE KNOW AND LOVE!

CAT-A-TONIC COMIC!

THE WORLD'S LONGEST RUNNING COMIC STRIP, WHICH BEGUN IN 1897, IS *THE KATZENJAMMER KIDS. KATZENJAMMER* MEANS *"YOWLING OF CATS"* IN GERMAN ...SLANG FOR *"HANGOVER!"*

Katzie cartoonist Rudolph Dirks and his friends.

HOW EAR-Y!

ANDY WARHOL DECLARED, *"MAD MAGAZINE* MADE ME FALL IN LOVE WITH PEOPLE WITH *BIG EARS!* THAT'S A *GOOD* INFLUENCE, ISN'T IT?"

Before.

After.

...BUT DEAN VISITED EVERY OTHER WEEKEND!

WHEN *DEAN MARTIN* AND *JERRY LEWIS* SPLIT UP, *JERRY LEWIS* GOT CUSTODY OF THE *COMIC BOOK!*

TRUTH OR HARE!

DARING TO COMPARE HERSELF TO *JESSICA RABBIT*, *MADONNA* SAID OF HER CHARACTER IN *DICK TRACY*, "SHE'S NOT BAD, SHE'S JUST *DRAWN THAT WAY!*"

UNDER THE INFLUENCE!

AMONG HIS INFLUENCES, ARTIST/CARTOONIST *ROBERT WILLIAMS* CITES *SALVADOR DALI, ROBERT CRUMB, X-RATED MOVIES, TITIAN, GANG GRAFFITI, GIRLIE MAGAZINES, TATTOO ART, TIJUANA BIBLES, HEINRICH KLEY,* AND *SKATEBOARD ART!*

Williams as seen by himself.

97

A Walker on the wild side, by Stan Drake.

BEETLE-MANIA!

AN ARMY OFFICER ONCE COMPLAINED, "THE *AIR FORCE* HAS *(STEVE) CANYON* AND THE *NAVY* HAS *(BUZZ) SAWYER...* WHAT'VE WE GOT? *BEETLE BAILEY!*"

QUIRKY QUOTES dept.

Drawn for *Weird but True* by Mort Walker.

CAT FIGHT!

PART I

NORMAN MAURER WROTE A SCENE FOR THE ANIMATED TV SHOW *JOSIE AND THE PUSSYCATS* IN WHICH A **PUSSYCAT**, ESCAPING FROM A MONSTER, HID IN A BOWL OF SPAGHETTI. A **CBS** EXECUTIVE **DEMANDED MAURER** CHANGE IT BECAUSE *"KIDS WILL PUT THEIR CATS IN SPAGHETTI!"*

An unpublished drawing by Dan DeCarlo, Josie's creator.

TO CRAIG YOE.. MY LONG TIME FRIEND.

Gary Larson's self-portrait.

Stigiphilus garylarsoni.

INSECTI-FAR SIDE!

GARY LARSON WAS HONORED BY *THE UNIVERSITY COMMITTEE ON EVOLUTIONARY BIOLOGY* WHEN THEY NAMED A SPECIES OF THE ORDER MALLOPHAGA (THE PARASITIC *"CHEWING LICE"*) INSECTS AFTER HIM! *WEIRD BUG TRUE!*

CAT FIGHT! PART 2

IN DIVORCE COURT, *LONI AND BURT'S* MOST *BITTER BATTLE* WAS FOUGHT OVER THEIR *$1,800 GARFIELD* SKETCH! *WEIRD BURT (AND LONI) TRUE!*

GET *DOWN!*

ANIMATION HISTORIANS *JOHN CAWLEY* AND *JIM KORKIS* CALL *DAFFY DUCK* THE MOST *"SEXUALLY ACTIVE"* TOON! *"DAFFY* WAS OFTEN MARRIED...MORE THAN ONCE HE WAS A HEN- (OR DUCK-) PECKED HUSBAND. HE EVEN HAD A *DIVORCE* DUE TO HIS CLOWNING AROUND THAT MADE (THE COUPLE'S) *EGG DISAPPEAR..."*

99

"ALL IS VANITY"

SKELE-TOON!

THIS *EERIE* DRAWING BY CARTOONIST *C. ALLAN GILBERT* DEPICTS THE *DEADLY* CONSEQUENCES OF *VANITY!*

DISNEY'S HARE LOSS!

DID *DISNEY* CREATE *WARNER BROS.' BUGS BUNNY?!* *WARNER'S* ANIMATOR *TEX AVERY* ADMITTED, "AS A DRAWING, *BUGS BUNNY* HAS AN AWFUL LOT IN COMMON WITH *MAX HARE* FROM *THE TORTOISE AND THE HARE,* ONE OF *WALT DISNEY'S SILLY SYMPHONIES. MR. DISNEY* WAS POLITE ENOUGH *NEVER TO MENTION IT!"*

Disney's Max Hare debuted in 1935.

Warner Bros.' Bugs Bunny had his start in the late '30's.

TOO DARN HOT!

THE RACY 1934 *BETTY BOOP* CARTOON *RED HOT MAMA* WAS *BANNED* IN ENGLAND BY THE *BRITISH BOARD OF CENSORS! WEIRD BUT BLUE!*

Hippie-era poster art by Victor Moscoso.

SEDUCTION OF THE INNOCENT dept.

HIGH-BEAMS!

IN HIS CALL FOR COMIC BOOK CENSORSHIP, *FREDRIC WERTHAM, M.D.,* DIRECTOR OF THE *MENTAL HYGIENE CLINIC OF BELLEVUE HOSPITAL,* GIVES US THIS LURID EXAMPLE OF WHAT HE CLAIMED CHILDREN CALL *"HEADLIGHTS"* COMICS!

PAINTIN' THE TOWN!

5 TONS OF SPECIAL PAINT, ALMOST *800 GALLONS,* WERE USED TO MAKE *101 DALMATIONS...* ENOUGH TO COAT *35 HOMES! WOOF BUT TRUE!*

"Shoe."

"John Q."

RIGHT ON "Q"

POLITICAL CARTOONIST *VAUGHN SHOEMAKER* PUT THE *"Q"* IN *JOHN Q. PUBLIC! WEIRD BUT "Q"!*

PETAL PUSHER!

WHEN *MIGHTY MOUSE* SNIFFED A FLOWER BEING SOLD BY *POLLY PINEBLOSSOM,* THE *REVEREND DONALD WILDMON* OF *THE AMERICAN FAMILY ASSOCIATION* PUBLICLY CHARGED *MIGHTY MOUSE* WITH *SNORTING COCAINE!*

INITIAL SUCCESS!

SUCCESSFUL CREATOR *MATT GROENING* HAS REVEALED HIS *INITIALS* ARE *HIDDEN* IN THE *HAIR* AND *EAR* OF *HOMER SIMPSON!*

102

AND IT WASN'T ABOUT THE *TIDY BOWL GUY!*

ON THIS *ARGENTINE* VERSION OF *THE FLASH* COMICS, THE TITLE WAS *INEXPLICABLY* CHANGED TO *FLUSH MAN!* *WEIRD BUT TRUE!*

Flush (right).

HE PIRATED THE IDEA!

MILTON CANIFF CREATED THE *SEXIEST* TOON VILLAINESS OF ALL TIME, *THE DRAGON LADY!* SHE WAS INSPIRED BY A *REAL* FEMALE PIRATE, *LAI CHOI SAN!*

THE ART OF ART!

CARTOONIST-GENIUS *ART SPIEGELMAN* WON A *PULITZER PRIZE* FOR HIS BOOK *MAUS*, IN WHICH *CATS* PLAYED THE PART OF *NAZIS* AND *MICE* PORTRAYED *JEWS!*

for craig w best wishes art spiegelman

EEK! A RAT!

FACT! *WALT DISNEY* BANNED THIS *MICKEY* DOLL, WHICH WAS MANUFACTURED IN ENGLAND, BECAUSE ITS *RAT-LIKE* APPEARANCE *FRIGHTENED* CHILDREN!

HAIR DU-O!

HIDDEN IN THIS *NIXON* CARICATURE BY *DAVID LEVINE* ARE TWIN SILHOUETTES OF *LBJ!*

Levine.

 dept.

AIRLIFTED!

Dilbert.

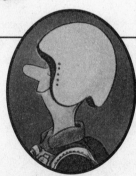

Dilbert.

DILBERT CREATOR *SCOTT ADAMS* ADMITS THAT *DILBERT'S* NAME WAS SUGGESTED BY HIS FRIEND, WHO LATER REALIZED HE'D *SUBCONSCIOUSLY* BORROWED IT FROM A *WWII* TOON BY *ROBERT OSBORN!* THE ORIGINAL *DILBERT* WAS AN INCOMPETENT NAVY PILOT USED TO SHOW PILOTING *DON'TS!*

the Bettie Page page!

quintuplet!
~~TWIN~~ A
T O O N S dept.

PHANTOM Lady
PRIZE
10¢
THIS ISSUE!
PHANTOM Lady
"THE SORE MENT KILLER!" "THE STINGING WHIP!"
A TRUE CRIME STORY
FRAMED by PHANTOM LADY!

Bettie Page.

Phantom Lady.

105

OW WW! ANYTHING FOR A PIN-UP!

Katy Keene.

Veronica.

Miss Lace.

ART IMITATES...DEATH!

1950'S HEALTH AND GOVERNMENT OFFICIALS *CRITICIZED* THE *CRIME DOES NOT PAY* COMIC BOOK FOR ACTUALLY *GLORIFYING CRIME.* BUT ARTIST/CO-EDITOR *BOB WOOD* PROUDLY PRINTED HIS NAME ON *EVERY COVER!* ON AUGUST 26, 1958, AFTER AN *11-DAY DRUNKEN LOVE TRYST* AT A HOTEL, *WOOD BLUDGEONED* HIS *GIRLFRIEND, MRS. VIOLETTE PHILLIPS,* TO *DEATH!* FOLLOWING HIS RELEASE FROM *SING-SING,* FORMER FELLOW INMATES *PUSHED WOOD* FROM A CAR TO A *GRISLY DEATH!*

In 1942, *Daredevil* #13 (unlucky title/number?) declared young Bob was "dripping with ambition."

106

DAILY NEWS 5¢

SLAYING ENDS 11-DAY TRYST

Artist Kills Woman in Hotel

"I Just Killed My Girl Friend."

16 years later, in a tryst of fate, Wood was dripping with the blood of his slain lover!

A RE-ENACTMENT OF THE MURDER DRAWN ESPECIALLY FOR *WEIRD BUT TRUE* BY AN ORIGINAL *CRIME DOES NOT PAY* ARTIST, *RUDY PALAIS!*

Did this comic book cover prophesy its editor's death when he was pushed from a car by thugs on the New Jersey Turnpike?

THE ROYAL FEAST OF BELSHAZZAR BLAINE AND THE MONEY KINGS.

TICKLE ME GROVER!

WALT McDOUGALL'S AND **VALERIAN GRIBAYEDOFF'S** FAMOUS CARTOON APPEARED JUST BEFORE *ELECTION DAY* IN 1884. HISTORIAN *STEPHEN BECKER* RECORDS IT HELPED "...SWING NEW YORK STATE – AND CONSEQUENTLY THE *PRESIDENTIAL ELECTION* – AWAY FROM *(JAMES) BLAINE* AND TO *(GROVER) CLEVELAND.*"

Gribayedoff and McDougall by Grant Wright, circa 1904.

I FEEL IT IN MY FINGERS, I FEEL IT IN MY TOES!

USING HIS *HANDS* AND *FEET*, TALENTED CARTOONIST *TOM BREEN* COULD DRAW *FOUR* CARTOONS AT THE *SAME TIME!*

107

HE PUT THE "HA" IN HANDICAPPED!

QUADRIPLEGIC CARTOONIST *JOHN CALLAHAN* BUILT HIS SUCCESSFUL BUT *POLITICALLY INCORRECT* CAREER ON POKING FUN AT THE HANDICAPPED! *MATT "THE SIMPSONS" GROENING* REMARKED, "RUDE, SHOCKING, DEPRAVED, TASTELESS... *CALLAHAN* GETS CALLED ALL THE ADJECTIVES CARTOONISTS *CRAVE TO HEAR!"*

CALLAHAN

A MEMBER OF THE WEBBING!

THIS SPECIAL *MARVEL COMICS* ISSUE ABOUT *SPIDER-MAN'S* MARRIAGE TO *MARY JANE WATSON* FEATURED A WEDDING DRESS DESIGNED BY FAMOUS FASHION DESIGNER *WILLI SMITH!*

Stan Lee (circa 1947) and Steve Ditko (circa 1966), the co-creators of Spider-Man.

HE WOULD HAVE BEEN HANDY IN **CHAPPAQUIDDICK, TOO!**

SAID *SENATOR TED KENNEDY,* "I DON'T THINK ANYONE...IN PUBLIC SERVICE HASN'T WISHED THEY COULD CALL ON *SUPERMAN* TO HELP IN A TIME OF *NATIONAL EMERGENCY. PRESIDENT KENNEDY* CERTAINLY WOULD HAVE ENJOYED HAVING HIM HANDY DURING THE *CUBAN MISSILE CRISIS!"*

An unpublished sketch by Joe Shuster, early 1940's.

Le Docteur Festus, one of Töpffer's groundbreaking comic books.

TEACHER'S PET PROJECT

MOST TEACHERS *CONFISCATE* COMIC BOOKS, BUT IN 1827, SWISS SCHOOL TEACHER *RODOLPHE TÖPFFER* (1799-1846) *INVENTED* POSSIBLY THE *VERY FIRST COMIC BOOK!*

109

Cruella de Vil animator Marc Davis.

SPEAK OF THE DE VIL!

A SURVEY OF *TOP ACTRESSES* REVEALS *CRUELLA DE VIL* IS *THE* MOST *BELOVED* MOVIE VILLAINESS! *SHARON STONE* GUSHED, "I LOVED *CRUELLA DE VIL* BECAUSE SHE HAD THE *BEST CHEEKBONES!"*

T⚥NVESTITES dept.

SO, WHICH ONE WAS IN TOUCH WITH HIS FEMININE SIDE?

HECKLE AND JECKLE BEGAN THEIR TOON CAREERS IN *THE TALKING MAGPIES* IN 1946 AS *HUSBAND* AND *WIFE!* *WEIRD BIRD TRUE!*

CEREAL AND O.J.!

O.J. SIMPSON PROSECUTOR *CHRISTOPHER DARDEN* WAS NICKNAMED *CRUNCHY*, AFTER *CAP'N CRUNCH*, DUE TO HIS PREMATURE *FALSE TEETH!*

110

"Gee, Pete, these glasses sure bring the Germans up close!"

WORLD WAR TOON dept.

THE JOE'S ON HIM!

PRIVATE *DAVE BREGER*, A REAL AMERICAN CARTOONIST, CREATED THE TERM AND TOON *G.I. JOE* DURING THE *BIG ONE!*

FRANKLY, MY DEAR, I DON'T GIVE A XⓄ☆#!!

CLARK KENT'S NAME WAS A COMBINATION OF THE NAMES OF ACTORS *CLARK GABLE* AND *KENT TAYLOR*!

DARTING INTO A STOREROOM, THE MILD-MANNERED NEWSMAN QUICKLY SHEDS HIS OUTER GARMENTS...

...TO BECOME-- SUPERMAN THE MAN OF STEEL!

celebrity cartoonist dept.

PSYCHIC CARTOON NETWORK!

CHER DREW THIS PROPHETIC SELF-PORTRAIT *JUST WEEKS* BEFORE EX-HUBBY *SONNY* FATALLY SKIED INTO A *TREE!*

111

WOOD YOU BELIEVE...

WALLY WOOD OF *WOODMERE*, N.Y., DREW WITH A *WOODEN* PENCIL ON A *WOODEN* TABLE. *WOOD'S* MOST BELOVED CHARACTER? *THE IRON MAIDEN!* *WOOD BUT TRUE!*

MY WORLD IS THE WORLD OF SCIENCE-FICTION... CONCEIVED IN MY MIND AND PLACED UPON PAPER WITH PENCIL AND INK AND BRUSH AND SWEAT AND A GREAT DEAL OF LOVE FOR MY WORLD. FOR I AM A SCIENCE-FICTION ARTIST. MY NAME IS WOOD.

MT. DUCKMORE!

A ROCK FORMATION NEAR MONO LAKE, CAL., *LOOKS EERILY* LIKE **DONALD DUCK!** *THE WORK OF DISNEY-WORSHIPPING ALIENS?!*

QUIRKY QUOTES dept.

To Yoe —.
YESH!
NO!

Patrick
·McDonnell·
©1998

"I MUTTS HAVE BEEN CRAZY!"

PATRICK McDONNELL, CARTOONIST OF THE COMIC STRIP *MUTTS,* REVEALS, "I'LL THINK UP AN IDEA, PENCIL IT, INK IT, AND PRONOUNCE MYSELF A *GENIUS.* THE NEXT DAY I'LL TAKE A PEEK AND ASK MYSELF *'WHAT'S THAT ABOUT?'"*

IS GRIFFITH GETTING ROYALTIES YET?

THE POPULAR PHRASE *"ARE WE HAVING FUN YET?"* ORIGINATED FROM THE LIPS OF *BILL GRIFFITH'S ZIPPY THE PINHEAD!*

Zippy's creator.

THE UNHAPPY HOOKER!

POLITICAL CARTOONIST *C. D. BATCHELOR* DARED TO PICTURE A *PROSTITUTE* IN THIS *NEW YORK DAILY NEWS* CARTOON IN 1937...BUT WON THE *PULITZER PRIZE* FOR HIS *ANTI-WAR STATEMENT!*

Pulitzer Prize material? The Most Eligible Batchelor by Odin Waugh, circa 1951.

"Come on in, I'll treat you right. I used to know your daddy."

HE'S TOAST!

FACT!

THE SLANG WORD *"MILQUETOAST"* CAME FROM THIS *WIMPY* CARTOON CHARACTER, *CASPAR MILQUETOAST,* CREATED BY *H.T. WEBSTER!*

Webster's definintion of himself, circa 1941.

MR. MILQUETOAST NEVER LIKES TO BE SEEN LOOKING AT UNDRAPED STATUARY

NICE PAIR OF **BOOPS!**

SINGER *HELEN KANE* THOUGHT *BETTY BOOP* LOOKED AND SOUNDED SUSPICIOUSLY IDENTICAL TO HERSELF! *KANE* SUED *FLEISCHER STUDIOS* AND *PARAMOUNT PICTURES* FOR $250,000!

HOW **UNORTHODOX!**

DURING THE HEIGHTH OF *TEEN-AGE MUTANT NINJA TURTLE* MANIA, SOME JEWISH BOYS SEWED *NINJA TURTLE* PATCHES ON THEIR *YARMULKES!*

114

TO CRAIG YOE

A daffy self-portrait.

FOR CRAIG
Chuck Jones

PAPER TRAINING!

ANIMATOR *CHUCK JONES* ATTRIBUTES HIS TALENT TO THE FACT THAT *EVERY TIME* HIS FATHER FAILED IN A NEW BUSINESS, HE WAS ENCOURAGED TO *DRAW WITH THE UNUSED STATIONERY* AND *PENCILS!* *WEIRD BUT DREW!*

YOU'VE *CRUMB* A LONG WAY, BABY!

R. CRUMB, ONE OF THE MOST *BRILLIANT* CARTOONISTS OF THIS *CENTURY*, FATHERED THE *UNDERGROUND COMICS* MOVEMENT BY SELLING HIS *ZAP COMIX* OUT OF A *BABY CARRIAGE* ON THE STREETS OF *HAIGHT-ASHBURY!*

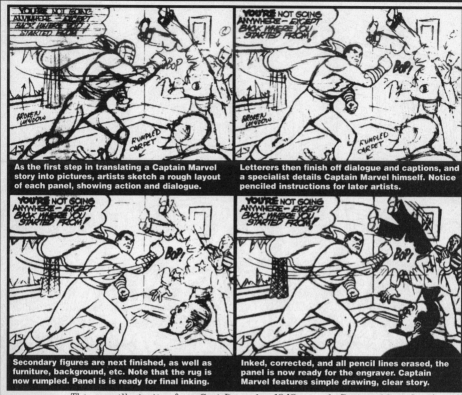

As the first step in translating a Captain Marvel story into pictures, artists sketch a rough layout of each panel, showing action and dialogue.

Letterers then finish off dialogue and captions, and a specialist details Captain Marvel himself. Notice penciled instructions for later artists.

Secondary figures are next finished, as well as furniture, background, etc. Note that the rug is now rumpled. Panel is is ready for final inking.

Inked, corrected, and all pencil lines erased, the panel is now ready for the engraver. Captain Marvel features simple drawing, clear story.

This rare illustration from *Spot*, December 1942, reveals Captain Marvel isn't real!

DID YOU EVER KNOW THAT YOU'RE MY SUPERHERO?

THE ARTISTS WHO DREW *CAPTAIN MARVEL* IN THE 1940'S WERE *FORBIDDEN* TO SIGN THEIR WORK. THEY WERE TOLD IT WAS *NOT TO UPSET* READERS WHO BELIEVED THE *SUPERHERO* WAS *REAL!*

THERE ONCE WAS A 'TOONIST NAMED LEAR...

WHO CAME FROM A FAMILY QUITE *QUEER.* HE HAD SIBLINGS *A-PLENTY,* IN ALL, THERE WERE *TWENTY,* AND THE *LIMERICK HE DID PIONEER!*

Free as a bard. . . Edward Lear.

A FLAMING LIE!

THE HUMAN TORCH, FROM COMIC BOOKS' *GOLDEN AGE*, WAS NOT A HUMAN, *BUT AN ANDROID!*

The Silver Age Torch *was* a human (drawn here by Dick Ayers)!

FLAME ON, CRAIG! YOUR PAL, DICK AYERS

A CRASH COURSE IN CARTOONING!

ZACK MOSLEY GOT THE IDEA FOR HIS AVIATION COMIC STRIP, *SMILIN' JACK*, WHEN A PLANE *CRASHED* IN HIS BACK YARD! *WEIRD* BUT THE IDEA *FLEW!*

Plane-looking Zack in a self-caricature.

I SOLD A PICTURE LAST WEEK FOR NINE DOLLARS AND BOUGHT THIS NEW SUIT OF CLOTHES. WITH THIS PICTURE I EXPECT TO PAY MY ROOM RENT

MANY HA-HA's!

COMIC ART AUTHORITY *ERNEST McGEE* CALLED *C.W. KAHLES* A *"GENIUS"* AND THE *"HARDEST-WORKING CARTOONIST* IN *HISTORY,* HAVING AS MANY AS *8* SUNDAY COMICS RUNNING AT *ONE TIME!"*

HOO-RAY FOR COMIC STRIPS!

LIFE WAS GOOD FOR *MILTON CANIFF*, BUT HE ALMOST WENT INTO *ACTING* INSTEAD OF DEVELOPING HIS SUCCESSFUL COMIC STRIPS *TERRY AND THE PIRATES* AND *STEVE CANYON*. YOUNG *CANIFF* HEEDED CARTOONIST *BILLY IRELAND'S* ADVICE TO HIM: "STICK TO YOUR INKPOTS, KID; *ACTORS DON'T EAT REGULARLY!*"

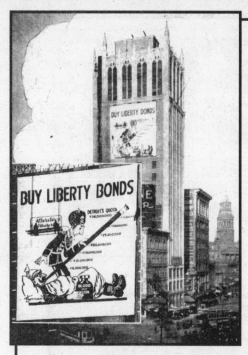

IT'S A **BIG** JOKE!

THIS *FIVE-STORY-TALL WW I* CARTOON WAS THE *LARGEST EVER* IN THE *WORLD!*

SMILE WHEN YOU SAY THAT!

HE WAS A *DISNEY* AND *WARNER BROS.* ANIMATOR WITH THE *PERFECT* NAME: *T. HEE!*

Ha ha!
T. Hee
by Chuck Jones.

HE'S IN THE **MIX!**

FULFILLING *MARVEL COMICS* WRITER *MARK GRUENWALD'S* DYING WISH, THE *ASHES* OF HIS *CREMATED CORPSE* WERE MIXED INTO THE INK USED TO PRINT THIS *SQUADRON SUPREME* COMIC BOOK! TALK ABOUT *GHOST WRITERS!*

EVERYBODY'S A CRITIC!

GAG CARTOONIST *GEORGE LICHTY* WAS *EXPELLED* FROM *THE CHICAGO ART INSTITUTE* AT THE AGE OF 18 FOR PLACING *GAG LINES* UNDER THE *REMBRANDTS* AND *EL GRECOS!*

A sample of Lichty's loose and luscious art.

A self-caricature.

"I WANT TO THANK THE LITTLE PIMPLE..."

FACT! SCOOBY-DOO STARRED IN THE EDUCATIONAL FILMSTRIP *THE SCOOBY-DOO GANG IN SKIN DEEP,* WHICH TASTEFULLY DEALT WITH THE SERIOUS SUBJECT OF *TEEN ACNE!*

Drawn especially for *Weird but True* by one of the original Scooby-Doodlers, Iwao Takamoto.

GETTING RICHIE!

WHEN PRODUCER *JOEL SILVER* OFFERED THE ROLE OF *RICHIE RICH* TO *MACAULAY CULKIN,* THE CHILD STAR SAID, "YOU WANT ME TO BE THIS," POINTING TO THE WORDS *"RICHIE RICH"* ON THE COMIC BOOK COVER. *CULKIN* THEN DEMANDED, "WE WANT *THIS,*" POINTING TO THE *REST* OF THE TITLE: *"MILLIONS"!*

Richie Rich MILLIONS

YOU'VE COME A LONG WAY, BOVEY!

IN AN EARLY *MICKEY MOUSE* CARTOON, CENSORS FOUND A COW'S *UDDERS* SO *SHOCKING* THAT *CLARABELLE COW* WAS FORCED TO WEAR A *DRESS*, THEREBY *SKIRTING* THE ISSUE! THAT'S A *FAR CRY* FROM TODAY'S *CARTOON NETWORK'S* *"COSMOPOLITOON"* COVER FEATURING A VERY SAUCY *"COW"*! *WEIRD BUT UDDERLY TRUE!*

IT'S A CINCH TO DRAW WITH THIS PENCIL

THE W.L.EVANS SYSTEM

Popeye's pappy, E.C. Segar.

COSMOPOLITOON

summer
**star
survey**

The No.1 Relationship
Mistake That Smart
Cows Make

style!
Cartoon Fashions
and Make-overs

**Escape
Your Shape**
Keep Your
Udders Perky

Confessions:
Toons that
Don't Wear
Pants and Why!

CARTOON
NETWORK

Lifestyles of
the Wives of
Really Famous
Toons

121

Rare Segar promotional art for Popeye animation.

CEREAL KILLER!

A COMMERCIAL STARRING TWO-FISTED *POPEYE* DECLARING *"CAN* THE SPINACH! I WANTS ME SOME *QUAKER INSTANT OATMEAL!"* WAS OBJECTED TO BY THE *QUAKERS,* WHOSE RELIGIOUS PRINCIPLES ARE BASED ON *NON-VIOLENCE.* THE *QUAKER* COMPANY *RE-DESIGNED THE CAMPAIGN!*

BLOW ME DOWN IF I AIN'T A BLARSTED MATINEE IDOL! ARF! ARF!

SPLAT

SO FUNNY I FORGOT TO LAUGH!

PAUL (TERRYTOONS) TERRY'S MOTTO: *"DISNEY* IS THE *TIFFANY'S* IN THIS BUSINESS, AND I AM THE *WOOLWORTH'S!"*

Terry's toon.

A THEATER OWNER TOLD *TERRY,* "WE RUN THE FEATURE AND THEN WE PUT ON A *TERRYTOON,* AND THAT DRIVES THE PEOPLE *OUT OF THE HOUSE!"*

122

©1991 Rick Griffin

DRAW UNTO ME!

CARTOONIST *RICK GRIFFIN* WAS A GUIDING FORCE IN PSYCHEDELIC POSTERS, ALBUM COVERS, THE SURF CULTURE AND *UNDERGROUND COMIX!* THIS SELF-PORTRAIT PICTURING *RICK* BEING WELCOMED BY AN ANGEL INTO HEAVEN'S DOOR WAS DRAWN AND PUBLISHED JUST BEFORE HIS *FATAL MOTORCYCLE ACCIDENT!*

HOLY TERROR!

CALVIN AND HOBBES BOOKS HAVE OUTSOLD THE *BIBLE* IN SOME STATES!

THEY WOULDN'T LET US...

SKINNY DIP FOR THE NEWSPAPERS

BUT WE'LL LET 'EM DO IT FOR THE SAN DIEGO COMIC-CON OF 1976

Self-portrait: Dahlia Messick.

The Brenda Starr strip.

123

STARR BILLING!

WHEN SHE CREATED *BRENDA STARR*, CARTOONIST *DAHLIA MESSICK* BILLED HERSELF AS *"DALE"* TO AVOID *PREJUDICE* AGAINST WOMEN CARTOONISTS!

JOIN, or DIE.

America's first political cartoon, from the *Pennsylvania Gazette*, May 9, 1754.

Franklin seen by fellow cartoonist Basil Wolverton.

YANKEE DOODLES!

BENJAMIN FRANKLIN WAS AMERICA'S *FIRST POLITICAL CARTOONIST!*

Mel and Bugs on
this Blanc page...

T^{he} LAST LAUGH...

MEL BLANC WAS HOLLYWOOD'S
"MAN OF A THOUSAND VOICES"!
HIS CHARACTERIZATIONS INCLUDED
*BUGS BUNNY, WOODY WOODPECKER,
DAFFY DUCK, BARNEY RUBBLE,*
AND THE FAMOUS *LOONEY TUNES* SIGN-OFF
WITH *PORKY PIG!*
MEL'S TOMBSTONE READS,

"THAT'S ALL FOLKS!"

FOR YOU LEGAL EAGLES

Scorchy Smith © AP Features; Hirschfeld art © Albert Hirschfeld; Elvis Presley photo © Alfred Wertheimer; Josie and the Pussycats, Katy Keene, Veronica © Archie Comics; Maus © Art Spiegelman; Miss Fury, Mutt and Jeff © Bell Syndicate, Inc.; Zippy © Bill Griffith; Calvin and Hobbes © Bill Watterson; Elsie the Cow © Borden's; Tintin, Snowy © Casterman; The Far Side © Chronicle Publishing Company; Chuck Jones art © Chuck Jones; South Park © Comedy Central; David Levine art © David Levine; Batgirl, Batman, Captain Marvel, Captain Marvel, Jr., Dean Martin and Jerry Lewis Comics, Flushman, The Joker, Lois Lane, The Penguin, Strange Adventures, Superman, Wonder Woman © DC Comics; 101 Dalmations, Clarabelle Cow, Cruella de Vil, Donald Duck, Dumbo, Fantasia, Gideon, Huey, Dewey, Louie, The Little Mermaid, Max Hare, Mickey Mouse, Minnie Mouse, Uncle Scrooge © Disney; Big Boy © Elias Brothers Restaurants, Inc.; Felix © Felix Comics, Inc.; Smokey Stover, Steve Canyon © Field Enterprises; Betty Boop © Fleischer Studios; Toonerville Trolley © Fontaine Fox; Fred Gwynne © Fred Gwynne Estate; Doonesbury © G. B. Trudeau; Sonny © General Mills; Little Lulu © Golden Books Publishing Company, Inc.; Clementine Cherie © Grayson Publishing Corp.; Valentina © Guido Crepax; Cow and Chicken, The Flintstones, The Jetsons, Scooby-Doo, Yogi Bear © Hanna-Barbera Productions, Inc.; Casper, Richie Rich © Harvey Cartoons; G.I. Joe © Hasbro; Punchie and Oaf © Hawaiian Punch; Hugh Hefner, Garfield © Jim Davis; John Callahan art © John Callahan; John Lennon © John Lennon's Estate; John Updike art © John Updike; Keith Harring art © Keith Harring; Tony the Tiger © Kellogg's; Barney Google, Beetle Bailey characters, Blondie and Dagwood, Bringing Up Father, G.I. Joe, Katzenjammer Kids, Henry, Krazy Kat, Mutts, Phantom, Polly and Her Pals, Popeye characters, Prince Valiant, Spark Plug © King Features Syndicate, Inc.; Barbarella © Le Terrain Vague & J.-C. Forest; Mad Magazine Boy's Head Device © EC Publications; Hulk, The Human Torch, Powerman, Spider-Man, Squadron Supreme © Marvel Entertainment Group, Inc.; Life in Hell © Matt Groening; Barbie © Mattel, Inc.; Joe Palooka © McNaught Syndicate, Inc.; Ding © Meredith Publishing Company; Miss Lace © Milton Caniff; Teenage Mutant Ninja Turtles © Mirage Studio; Eggbert © Monogram of California; Paul McCartney art © MPL Communications, Inc.; Beavis and Butthead © MTV Network; Buck Rogers © National Newspaper Syndicate; Eek and Meek © NEA; Batchelor art © New York Daily News; Caspar Milquetoast © The New York Herald Tribune, Inc.; Charles Addams art, James Thurber art © New Yorker Magazine, Inc.; Little Orphan Annie, Terry and the Pirates © News Syndicate Co., Inc.;

I'M JUST SUPER**MOUSE!** I COULD NEVER OUT-SUPER **CRAIG-YOE!**

Best Wishes Don Arr Christensen '83

Supermouse by one of his original 1940's artists, Don Arr.

MIGHT MAKES *RIGHT!*

IN HIS FIRST CARTOON *MIGHTY MOUSE* WAS CALLED *SUPERMOUSE!* CONTRARY TO POPULAR BELIEF, IT WASN'T THE *SUPERMAN LAWYERS* WHO MESSED WITH THE RODENT'S NAME. THERE WERE *COPYRIGHT PROBLEMS* WITH AN OBSCURE COMIC BOOK PUBLISHER WITH A CHEESE-LOVING HERO NAMED *SUPERMOUSE!*

Mighty Mouse.

Pokemon © Nintendo; Three Stooges © Norman Maurer Productions and Columbia Pictures; Astro Boy © Osamu Tezuka; Mr. Peanut © Planter's Peanuts; Brother Juniper © Publishers Syndicate; R. Crumb art © R. Crumb; Family Circus © Register and Tribune Syndicate; Rick Griffin art © Rick Griffin; Ripley art and photo © Ripley Entertainment, Inc.; Robert Nilson art © Robert Nilson; Robert Williams art © Robert Williams; Rudolph the Red-Nosed Reindeer © The Rudolph Company L.C.; Rock Hudson photo © Sid Avery/MPTV; Nutty the Friendly Dump © Spumco; Yellow Submarine © Subafilms Limited/© Apple Corps Limited; Bazooka Joe © Topps; Jessica Rabbit, Roger Rabbit © Touchstone Pictures & Amblin Entertainment, Inc.; Brenda Starr, Dick Tracy, Dondi, The Gumps, The Mole, Moon Mullins © Tribune Media Services, Inc.; Red, Tom & Jerry © Turner Entertainment Co.; Mighty Mouse, Polly Pineblossom, The Simpsons © Twentieth Century Fox; Alley Oop, Li'l Abner, Nancy characters, Peanuts characters © United Media Services; Dilbert © United Feature Syndicate; Willie and Joe © United Feature Syndicate/Bill Mauldin; Mr. Magoo © UPA; Heckle and Jeckle © Viacom International; VIP art © VIP Estate; Pogo © Walt Kelly; Woody Woodpecker © Walter Lantz; Boris, Bullwinkle, Natasha, Rocky © Ward Productions, Inc.; Bugs Bunny, Duffy Duck, Elmer Fudd, Pepe Le Pew, Porky Pig, Road Runner, Tweety © Warner Bros.; Herblock © Washington Post; The Spirit © Will Eisner; Wally Wood art © William M. Gaines, Agent, Inc.; Wolverton Art © Wolverton Estate.

THANK YOU!

A TIP OF THE HATLO HAT

Much thanx to Clizia Gussoni! As my partner in YOE! Studio, she never questioned the idea of the proceeds of this book going to charity and the studio spending the thousands of unpaid hours needed to realize this toon-tome. Her good ear for language, her great eye for design, her Gussoni sense of humor, and her giant heart for toons made this book sound, look, and feel immensely better.

And a big thanx to these others at YOE! Studio: Jayne Antipow, Danielle Antonini, Joy Court, Karen Finkel, Zakima Goldsmith, Nerio Gussoni, Rosalie Lent, Barbara Lipp, Luke McDonnell, Dan Merson, Jessica Murdock, Gene Murphy, Rob Penner, Mary Jane Ryan, Renee Rizzo, Jim Sheeran, Timothy Wood and everyone else who, while busy with their own projects, were always happy to offer valuable suggestions.

These fellow historians fact-checked the book: Jerry Beck, Bill Blackbeard, John Canemaker, Ron Goulart, R. C. Harvey, Alan Kaplan, Mark Kausler, Richard Marschall, Richard West. I'm indebted to them for their time and credit them for the book's accuracy (any mistakes are all mine and will be corrected in future editions). Thanx to David Smith of the Disney Archives for his fact checking, too.

I'd like to thank my editor at Random House, Greg Suriano, for his enthusiasm for the material and long-suffering patience while I took my own sweet time to make this book as perfect as I knew how.

The first editor to print a few of my weird factoids was Maggie Thompson, in the pages of *Comics Buyer's Guide*. Thank you, Maggie!

Love to Avarelle, Donovan, Valissa, Astrella, and Jean Ann.

126

THE GRATEFUL DUDES!

THEIR PHRASES, *"AFTER YOU, DEAR ALPHONSE. NO, AFTER YOU, DEAR GASTON."* ARE PART OF THE LANGUAGE! *FREDERIC OPPER'S* CHARACTERS HAVE BEEN CALLED *"NATIONAL SYMBOLS"* OF *"UNBOUNDED POLITESSE."*

Opper draws an editor (left) and himself for *Puck* in 1848.

A deep thanx to the many wonderful cartoonists who drew special drawings and to my friend Alice Davis.

WORLDWIDE WEB SLINGERS

Visit the *Weird but True* web site at www.weirdbuttrue.com for facts behind the facts and late-breaking amazements as they become available.

TO BE CONTINUED...

In the future there will be a *Son of Weird but True Toon Factoids*. If you have factoids, quirky quotes, twin toons, pictures of toonvestites, rare art (for loan—or better yet, for sale), etc., please contact us at yoestudi@cloud9.net.

WEIRD BIO TRUE!

JIM HENSON WAS A REAL CUT-UP

Craig Yoe was a Creative Director and Vice President/General Manager of the Muppets! Jim Henson declared, "Craig brings with him his valuable creativity and enthusiasm. He has a nice mix of business and creative talent."
Fact! Jim created Kermit by cutting up his mother's coat!

A MOUNTAINTOP EXPERIENCE

Craig and his partner, Clizia Gussoni, run YOE! Studio in a castle atop a mountain overlooking the Hudson River. YOE! Studio creates everything from toothbrushes to theme parks, characters to comic books, radios to race cars, apparel to animation! YOE! Studio has worked with more toons than anyone else in the world: from Superman to South Park, Spider-Man to Snoopy, Betty Boop to Batman.

WE'RE TALKING BIG

Craig was responsible for the redesign of Big Boy and the Boy's comic book—the highest circulated comic book in the world!

...AND WE'RE NOT JUST BLOWING BUBBLES

Craig was also responsible for the redesign of Bazooka Joe and Joe's new comic strips. These strips are the widest read in the world!

HOW TOON

The how-to-draw-cartoons books Craig designed for the Cartoon Network and Post Cereals taught over 100 million people how to create cartoons, making him the biggest toon teacher in history!

TALKING 'BOUT THE MTV G-G-GENERATION

The station ID Craig created for MTV debuted on the MTV Award Show to 80 countries and went on to win numerous international awards...yet was finished just moments before its inaugural broadcast!

MIGHTY MICKEY MOUSE

The author's award-winning book *The Art of Mickey Mouse* (with an introduction by John Updike) is printed in four languages: French, German, Japanese, and of course, English. Disney CEO Michael Eisner personally gave a copy to the Pope.

MUSEUM QUALITY

Craig has been a consultant on toons to the Smithsonian Institution and the *New York Times*, and for books like *Ron Goulart's Great History of Comic Books*. Craig has exhibited his collection of rare art and has appeared at cartoon conventions around the world, in San Diego, California, Lucca, Italy, and southern France.

A rare self-caricature of *Nancy*'s Ernie Bushmiller.

Weird but through!